Anger Management for Children and Teens

Dunstamac

Published by Dunstamac, 2022.

Table of Contents

(This page is intentionally blank)

Introduction

When a child begins to grow, they are exposed to issues that often spiral out of control. They may have anger that manifests in the most antisocial manner.

As a child begins to comprehend the world of adolescence, there are many confusions and chaos, which can occasionally affect their growth. Many factors can contribute to a child's body and mind becoming out of control throughout the shift. This may develop into anger if not properly guided.

Parents and educators must educate children about the various transitional changes that will occur in their bodies. Regrettably it is during these years that children meet some of the most difficult situations. This stage of a teen's life can expose them to different events, which can be unpleasant.

Teens in today's world are more susceptible to pressures than teens in the past. They face an increased risk of violence and hatred. Other teenagers may come from dysfunctional families where domestic abuse is a daily occurrence.

When teenagers are perplexed, they may react indifferently. Teenagers between the ages of twelve and sixteen are more likely to do things their way because they believe their emotions and independence are being restricted; this may result in mismanaged anger.

Teenagers tend to lash out when confronted with an unpleasant scenario. Teenagers often adopt a careless attitude during their youth. As a result, parents need to assist teens with anger management to reclaim control over their raging emotions.

Coping with the many situations that constantly present themselves can be emotionally draining for a teenager. This results in stress and anger. When a situation becomes complicated, anger might be a normal reaction.

However, it is how an individual responds to these feelings that make a difference. Teens can learn about self-awareness and self-control through anger management. As anger is such a strong emotion, it can cause many harm and grief if handled carelessly. As a result, it can be confidently asserted that developing the ability to manage one's anger from a young age can benefit one's adult life.

Teens should be encouraged to pay attention to their emotions during times of stress. It will help them understand that pausing for a second before acting can significantly impact how someone performs. A teenager who is easily upset needs self-control training. Children must learn to think before they act, as this will undoubtedly have a favourable influence.

Self-awareness and self-control are important components of anger management. For it is self-evident that pausing to consider their anger will have a restraining influence on their actions. There are many services available to assist youngsters in gaining control of their anger. Teaching teenage children anger management skills is not easy, but it can be quite rewarding once accomplished.

If the situation becomes intolerable, the minors' guardians or the teens themselves may seek professional aid and many would agree that effective hypnosis can significantly assist them in this endeavour.

Anger management classes can also be extremely beneficial for these troubled adolescents. This specialized program teaches children how to modify their behaviour in more acceptable ways. They will learn to think positively, particularly if their families do not model good reactions to challenges. They can now learn how to deal with challenging emotions as a result.

Managing anger is fundamentally about empowerment, appraising the situation and making informed choices rather than behaving rashly on impulse. It is so natural to strike out at the mere sight of opposition but it requires tremendous self-control to remain rational and act logically in such a scenario.

This may appear to be an impossible undertaking for a child, but it is possible with the proper anger management strategies. Teaching a teenager anger management techniques requires instilling a sense of self-awareness; it entails demonstrating that they can assess a situation and act maturely rather than lashing out on impulse.

Happy Reading

(This page is intentionally blank)

Chapter 1

What is Anger?

Anger is a strong emotion of disagreement generated by some kind of complaint which is either actual or thought by a person to be true. The cognitive hypothesis of conduct relates coldness to several reasons, including as past experience, behaviour learnt from others, genetic predispositions and lack of problem solving.

Likewise, anger is the result of a combination of two factors: an unreasonable vision of reality ("It must be done my way") and a low frustration threshold ("It must be done my way or else"). Anger is an internal reaction to an external stimulus that is considered to have a cause.

Almost usually, angry people blame their reactions on some person or incident, but they rarely recognize that their anger results from their illogical vision of the world. Angry people have a preconceived notion and expectation of the world they live in, and when that reality falls short of their expectations, they become furious.

It's critical to recognize that not all anger is unhealthy. Anger is one of our most primal protection mechanisms, defending and motivating us against external dominance or manipulation.

It provides us with the additional power, courage, and determination necessary to fight injustice perpetrated against us or others we care about. However, if anger is allowed to run wild and seize control of the mind and body at any time, it becomes harmful.

Just as a person under the influence of a street drug is unable to rationalize, comprehend, or make sound decisions, a person under the influence of anger cannot rationalize, comprehend, or make sound decisions because anger twists logical thought into blind emotion.

You lose your ability to reason logically, and your emotions take over your actions. Anger activates our brain's fight or flight reaction, raising our blood pressure and releasing adrenaline into our bloodstream, enhancing our power and pain threshold. Anger compels us to act in two ways:

(1) Defend or

(2) Attack.

Neither of these approaches promotes effective negotiating. Anger's Internal Sources

Internal roots of anger originate in our faulty interpretations of reality. Psychologists have identified four distinct modes of thought that contribute to the development of anger.

- Emotional deliberation.

Individuals who reason emotionally perceive everyday events and statements made by others as direct threats to their needs and aspirations.

Individuals who utilize emotional reasoning are prone to become annoyed by seemingly innocuous statements made by others because they view them as an attack on themselves. In the long run, emotional thinking might result in dysfunctional wrath.

- Low tolerance for frustration.

We had all encountered times in our lives when our tolerance for frustration was low. Often, anxiety caused by stress reduces our tolerance for irritation, and we tend to interpret everyday events as threats to our well-being or ego.

- Imprudent expectations.

When individuals make demands, they perceive things in terms of how they should be, rather than how they are. This reduces their tolerance for frustration, as individuals with excessive expectations expect others to behave a specific way or for uncontrollable circumstances to behave predictably. When these events do not unfold as planned, anger, frustration, and ultimately despair set in.

- Ratings by the public.

People-rating is an anger-inducing mode of thought in which one individual assigns a pejorative name to another. By labelling someone a "bitch" or a "bastard," you dehumanize them and make it easier to feel infuriated with them.

External Sources Of Anger

Hundreds of internal and external events can furious us, but given the constraints of negotiation, we can narrow these causes down to four broad categories.

1. The individual launches personal attacks on us. The other side verbally abuses you in addition to the issue.

2. The individual criticizes our ideas. The opposing side stifles our ideas, beliefs, and choices.

3. The individual poses a threat to our needs. The individual threatens to deprive us of a fundamental need if they do not get their way, e.g., "I'll ensure you never work in this city again."

4. We become irritable. Our tolerance for completing tasks may be poor or influenced by various contextual conditions in our life.

Factors That Reduce Our Tolerance for Frustration

- Anxiety / Stress.

Our tolerance for frustration reduces as our stress level rises. This explains why there are so many domestic conflicts and divorces caused by financial difficulties.

- Agony.

Our tolerance for irritation decreases as a result of physical and mental discomfort. This is because we are so preoccupied with meeting our basic survival requirements that we have no time for anything or anyone else.

- Substance abuse/alcoholism.

Drugs and alcohol alter the way our brain processes information, increasing a person's irritability or bringing previously suppressed emotions or memories to the surface, which can induce anger.

- Recent annoyances.

Recent annoyances might also be referred to as "having a horrible day." The small irritations that accumulate during the day reduce our tolerance for frustration. Recent annoyances may include stumbling in a puddle, spilling coffee on your shirt, being late for work, getting stopped in traffic, or getting a flat tire.

Recognizing Anger's Physiological Signs

By recognizing the physiological indications of anger, we may train ourselves to recognize when to take action to keep our anger under control. The following are some signs of anger:

1. Unconscious muscle tenseness, particularly in the face and neck.

2. Grinding of the teeth

3. The rate of respiration increases considerably.

4. Due to a rise in blood pressure, the face becomes red and veins become evident.

5. The face becomes pallid

6. Perspiring

7. Sensation of heat or chill

8. Hand-shaking

9. Goosebumps

10. Increased heart rate

11. Adrenaline is released into your system, increasing energy.

Am I Correct In Being Angry?

You are correct. You have your perceptions and expectations of the world you live in, and when reality falls short of those expectations, you have a right to feel upset. After all, if everyone thought the same way, the world would be quite dull. You're going to encounter unpleasant situations. You will come across individuals that do not respect your thoughts and ideas. Your anger is completely justified in light of your convictions; thus, do not suppress or ignore those feelings.

Having the right to be furious does not imply that you have the right to lash out at the other person in anger. You cannot coerce other people's beliefs into conforming to your own since they have the right to maintain their perspective of the world like you. The best action is to acknowledge your anger and direct it into the issue at hand rather than toward your adversary.

Significant Points

Getting furious or annoyed is analogous to being high on a drug. It impairs your ability to reason and think logically.

Anger is a state of mind characterized by an unreasonable sense of reality and a low frustration threshold. While anger is a normal response and you have every right to be furious, you must learn to control your anger during a negotiation because reacting to a negotiation results in the loss of the agreement.

Anger is a universal emotion shared by children and adults. When something or someone negatively affects an individual, they may get furious. Anger is a natural reaction to this type of event. Anger, on the other hand, might be classified as a mild or severe irritant. Anger can drive a person to become irritated or furious depending on the individual, the event and their emotions.

While anger is a natural and healthy emotion, there is a serious problem when it takes over an individual's life, causing them to be destructive and violent. Not only does anger ruin the individual, but it also affects everyone and everything in their immediate vicinity. Anger management can be able to transform these individuals and restore them to a healthy, normal life.

When people are angry, they behave differently: some lash out, others become extremely defensive; others keep their anger to themselves, burying their bad sentiments and hurt; and still others lose control and become violent. Without control, anger can create some quite difficult circumstances.

Thus, controlling one's anger is important. The first step toward resolving anger issues is to acknowledge that they exist. Some individuals who have significant anger issues cannot see it. Individuals who struggle with owning their anger and accepting responsibility for their actions often blame other things and people.

They refuse to contemplate the possibility that a situation becomes problematic due to their actions. They are constantly looking for something or someone to blame. Some want anger management courses immediately and urgently.

Often, persons who struggle with anger take offense when anger management is proposed. This refusal to admit their dilemma stops people from receiving the assistance they require.

If a person is consistently acting out and is furious, it will eventually result in severe difficulties. Without effective anger management, a person's personal or professional life may suffer.

It must be made plain to a person struggling with such issues that anger management is not a punishment but a means of assisting them in living a better life. It is a means to assist them in identifying their issues, addressing them and eventually resolving them.

Also, it trains individuals to liberate themselves from the dictates of their emotions, particularly their anger. Anger management is designed to teach a person how to control their anger in any situation.

There are many methods for controlling one's anger. There are specific programs designed to assist folks who struggle with severe anger issues. These programs are segmented to address the unique requirements of children, adolescents, adults, couples and families. All these tactics are geared toward teaching people how to resolve conflicts and manage their anger.

Without anger management, this individual will likely suffer loss, including family, work, and self-identity. It is important to convince the individual struggling with anger that anger management is not intended as a punishment but rather to improve their quality of life. Anger management is intended to assist the individual in resolving their issues, in determining why they feel upset.

Also, it teaches the individual not to be enslaved by their emotions, particularly their anger. Anger management is intended to teach the individual strategies to prevent them from being angry as often or for as long.

Chapter 2

Why Does Your Teen Become Angry and Depressed?

Parenting is a roller coaster ride. Occasionally, there are moments of joy and pleasure and the process appears to be difficult and painful. Parents' entire lives revolve around caring for and safeguarding their children. Nonetheless, this generation's children are impatient, frustrated and furious.

Every other family has experienced the scenario where children drive their parents insane with their demands and tantrums. Regardless of all the comforts and love, children moan and show their anger about various things.

Anger is not a negative emotion in and of itself. As with joy, sorrow and suffering, anger is a natural human emotion. Indeed, it is the manner of expression that aggravates the situation.

When children fight with their siblings, they may injure themselves. In some instances, they will strike and bite their friends at the least provocation. Teenagers may even verbally abuse their parents, destroy property and flee their homes in anger.

As previously said, anger is a natural emotion but when expressed in an abusive or violent manner, it can also result in undesired and unexpected effects. Uncontrolled anger in children can result in the following:

- Complaints from neighbours and instructors are increasing
- Confrontations with siblings and friends
- Public embarrassment for parents

- Social boycott and the furious child's rejection
- Injuries sustained by the child or others
- Adult incapacity to control and manage anger
- Relationships with parents and family were ruined.

These heinous outcomes are enough to keep parents awake at night. Also, a child with such a behavioural condition cannot live a healthy and happy life in society.

Who is to blame for children's developing anger?

No, children are not as accountable as adults. It is their environment that trains them to intensify their anger and let it erupt like a bomb. Often, children learn to show their anger in inappropriate ways from their parents.

They pay close attention to the parents' reactions in harsh and negative conditions. They observe their parent's anger, scream, toss objects, use inappropriate language, slam doors and occasionally engage in vicious bickering when their expectations are not realized.

Parents serve as role models for children and their behaviour establishes a pattern for how children show their anger. Children receive their first anger management tips from their parents and family members! As a result, it is up to parents and families to teach children how to resolve conflicts amicably.

Adolescent anger is becoming a much more severe issue in our society. We have all heard stories about angry teenagers becoming increasingly upset with life, which manifests as anger.

As a child progresses through puberty and into adulthood, their hormone levels fluctuate dramatically. As they develop, this hormonal imbalance is what contributes to moody adolescents. They can be happy one day and miserable the next.

While this is difficult for us grownups to comprehend and deal with, we were once there. It is confusing for the child who is going through it. They are too grown and old to play children's games and use children's toys but too immature to be treated as adults and do adult functions.

It is important to engage in teenage anger management, as teen anger can spiral out of control quickly. A random outburst in response to a harmless request can quickly escalate into violence and worse if you do not have an adolescent anger management strategy in place.

Today's teenagers are under greater pressure than we had in our childhood. They have witnessed thousands of killings and a lot of violence on television and computer games by the time they reach the age of eighteen. To a large number of them, this degree of violence is considered normal. The surge in divorce has sparked outrage among children caught in the crossfire between mom and dad.

If you have a child who struggles with anger, you must assert control but in a way that demonstrates empathy without being condescending.

Teenagers in tribal societies and the past underwent a rite of passage to mark their entry into adulthood. This rite of passage is no longer a part of our "civilized" civilizations in the way that we assume it was. Still, this distinction between child and adult is important for the child to understand their place in society.

Our culture has a tendency to swaddle children in cotton wool out of concern for their safety and well-being but we often go too far and deprive them of life experiences. This cotton wool mentality further blurs and delays the line between child and adult, implying that the youngster has no concept of who they are.

While outbursts of anger and resentment are not abnormal, they can develop into awful behaviours in how a child or young person communicates that anger over time.

While anger expressions are not uncommon in children, it is during this formative stage that lifelong anger patterns can develop if a program to manage the anger is not established.

It is crucial to teach youngsters how to process and express negative emotions such as anger appropriately. Conditioning youngsters to control their anger from an early age is important for developing the child's intellect.

When dealing with adolescent anger, parents must be disciplined and firm in responding to the adolescent's violence. The parent must be an effective communicator to gain insight into the child's difficulties outside the house.

Parents must be supportive and sympathetic when they notice their child is unhappy, as the parent's ignorance of the issue will exacerbate the child's distress. Also, the parent must communicate with the child, offering appropriate ways to deal with and express their anger.

Positive reinforcement is an effective strategy for taming angry outbursts and undesirable tantrums. Reward the child for exercising self-control and managing their anger appropriately. By rewarding youngsters for restraining their outbursts, they will learn acceptable methods of anger management.

Remind children that self-control is important by offering unique privileges after a period of appropriate behaviour. Take away the child's special advantages if they express themselves in an inappropriate manner, such as through violence or vulgarity.

When a child's angry outbursts escalate into physical aggressiveness that threatens to damage another person, seeking help from an anger management program is essential. Even if the anger manifests as destructive conduct, most people consider any bodily manifestation of anger unacceptable.

At this time, locating a professional program to assist your adolescent in coping with the anger will have a lasting effect on how the adolescent handles the anger. By addressing and resolving the anger at an early age, you can rescue your child from a lifetime of issues with anger.

If your adolescent has anger difficulties, you must intervene before they become a significant problem. Engage children in groups that are beneficial to them (not gangs) and encourage them to engage.

Begin by assigning them some responsibility and assisting them in navigating the tough journey to maturity. Assist them in developing into adults and treat them accordingly when appropriate.

With the surge in teen anger, adolescent anger management is important. You don't want your child to get into trouble at school or with the police, so you must address and resolve any anger issues early on.

(This page is intentionally blank)

Chapter 3

Recognizing The Early Signs Of Anger In Children

Reasons Why You Should Check For Signs Early!

While anger is a natural emotion, it must be dealt with appropriately constructively for healthy existence. Couples fighting, abusive parents beating children or teenagers being impatient and disrespectful toward authority authorities are all common examples of strong anger. Yet, even children - little ones are impacted by high feelings of anger.

Anger in very young children is difficult to recognize because it requires close observation; extremely few children cannot express their feelings. Their outbursts are misinterpreted as temper tantrums when they cannot verbalize their emotions.

A small child requesting something in a mall may throw a tantrum and while this can be painful for both parents and child, disregarding this type of behaviour - as is sometimes done - is not the way to cope with it. Being a child does not excuse bad behaviour and even angry children must be taught about the consequences of unpleasant, undesirable behaviour.

A child's upbringing must include guidance, tolerance and patient discipline toward desirable behaviour by emphasizing a value system and appreciating and acknowledging desirable behaviour; because children learn what is good and bad at a young age, they must also be directed in the direction of becoming healthy adolescents and adults, including the ability to control their temper.

Anger management programs are specifically designed to ascertain the root cause of a child's anger issue, as each child is unique and thus treatment must be tailored accordingly; this necessitates that the program focus on a specific area for one child, another for the second and so on, utilizing multiple methods for determining the nagging issue.

Some children respond angrily, others remain mute or uncommunicative, and others conceal their inner thoughts; in all situations, time is important for comprehending, diagnosing, and resolving the quest for suitable responses to anger-related concerns.

Engage young children in anger management awareness by providing them with activity papers that include colouring pages, quizzes, puzzles and circumstances that need optimum behaviour responses when they place themselves in the settings stated or illustrated.

They are intended to be a play-based method for effectively teaching children anger management skills by occupying their attention long enough to deal with the issue subtly and instilling better values such as sharing, using toys in turn and remaining polite even when disagreeing.

Thus, games and worksheets based on potentially heated scenarios for children are effective strategies to teach them about anger control without the youngsters being aware that their issue is being analysed and handled.

For older children who are willing to verbalize their feelings, it is a good idea to take them to counsel on this subject and build trust and comfort levels so they can bring their innermost feelings to the surface to figure out the best way to deal with situations and people that make them angry, in addition to teaching them how to deal with anger effectively and positively.

They can be asked to write or draw the angry situation or reaction to convey the pain, frustration and embarrassment associated with an angry situation. Reminding them that asking for help is not bad is an excellent way to ensure that anger management techniques work for both younger and older children.

In many homes, a teen's anger is a frequent source of contention between parents and teens. Being a teen is all about the desire for more independence, which entails questioning or rejecting their parent's authority's norms and demands.

Parents often become upset and furious due to being questioned and attempting to maintain communication. Adolescence is difficult for parents because they have spent years raising their children only to let them go gradually.

Anger and frustration often manifest themselves as violence in the form of a verbal, emotional or physical conflict. Teenagers typically become furious when they believe their parents are ordering them around, accusing them or lecturing them.

Teens' tempers might also flare when they believe their parents are continually bothering them, criticizing them or their friends, denying them solitude or trust and showing preference toward another sibling. Among the earlier concerns made by teenagers about their parents is that they are unresponsive or purposefully embarrass them in front of their friends.

The following are ways for identifying a teen's anger:

1. It is not primarily an issue of anger. Recognize that your teen's anger is only the surface and that more sensitive feelings often lurk beneath their furious or aggressive outburst.

Anger is typically a transitory emotion that masks injured sentiments and it provides an opportunity to practice resolving conflicts and being more empathetic with others. It's beneficial to constantly inquire the furious teen, "What else are you feeling besides anger?"

Usually, more delicate emotions lurk beneath the anger and they're worth talking about, such as how they're feeling hurt, frightened, frustrated, puzzled and uncertain and shame and regret. Teens are more prone to be furious when exhausted or hungry, ill, preoccupied or overloaded by homework or social events.

2. Inspire your teen to focus on their perspective on the situation. Assist them in seeing that it is the response, not the emotion that matters most. Because anger can exacerbate unfavourable thoughts about a problem, it can also cloud their judgment over how to address the matter.

Sometimes things are intricate and when one is in great anger, a misunderstanding is overlooked or oversimplified. Nobody can compel them to act out without their relinquishing control.

When adolescents become upset, it is normal for them to perceive the worst in others and assume that everyone is against them or that something was done on purpose. At that point, they are almost certainly in excruciating pain. Consider it further and recognize that not everyone is out to get them helps alleviate the anger.

3. Teens cannot be furious without being concerned. If a teen shouts "Whatever!" or "I don't care!" their response communicates more than their words. Individuals become furious over issues that matter to them.

As a parent, it is often worthwhile to discuss the concerns that are most important to them. It's simpler to listen to and discuss when parents recognize the significance of an issue rather than accuse them of wrongdoing. "What counts to me is that when you failed to deliver on your promises, I felt dissatisfied and cannot rely on you."

Allow them time alone to let off steam through exercise or being given space to calm down. Consider their perspective through the lens of what they are truly seeking, which is a balance between their desire for increased freedom and your desire for them to be responsible. Assist them by urging them to prioritize their values and ways to mend or improve the relationship or circumstance.

(This page is intentionally blank)

Chapter 4

Parents, Are You a Yelling Person?

A parent writes, "Our family is having difficulty deciding on suitable consequences when our teenager violates family rules." There's no way of knowing whether we are too tough or too forgiving. What are our options?"

This appears to be a point of contention for many parents. The issue of proper punishment and consequences is important. Now take note that I mentioned punishment and consequences, not punishment alone. This is because I believe an important distinction should be made.

The distinction is in our objective when responding to unwanted and improper behaviour.

If the goal is to express our anger, dominate the adolescent and elicit resentment, then punishment is the way to proceed. On the other hand, if our purpose is to communicate clearly, control and guide the adolescent, and impart life lessons, consequences are the way to go.

Consequences for behaviour are used to teach children about the real world.

In general, there are two types of consequences: natural and logical. Natural consequences occur due to one's actions and decisions. If we run red lights in the adult world, we risk being hit and injured; if we miss work without justification, we risk being fired. Allowing natural consequences to emerge is sometimes far too difficult in the world of children. A parent should never permit the inevitable consequences of running into a busy street.

When natural consequences become too harmful, it is necessary to impose logical consequences.

Generally, these entail some reduction in privileges due to reckless action. When structuring acceptable logical consequences, I employ two general models.

There exist three R's of logical consequences: related, respectful and reasonable.

Related: The term "related" merely refers to the activity. If a child breaches their curfew, forcing them to stay late at school or mow the lawn is irrelevant. This is connected to the temporary loss of the privilege of going out.

Respectful: We want to avoid two things here: embarrassing the adolescent and inconveniencing the adult.

Reasonable: It is irrational to say that you are grounded for life and will never see the light of day again. It is plausible to conclude that your behaviour and decisions have resulted in you losing the privilege of going out tomorrow night.

I've added three S's to these three R's: strong, swift and short-term.

Strong: "Honey, I truly wish you would refrain from coming in so many hours past your curfew" is not strong enough. The temptation to skip out on the next opportunity is tremendous.

Swift: Adults and adolescents have distinct perceptions of time. As grownups, we understand that we need to start immediately if a project is due two months. For many adolescents, two months equates to an eternity, which results in a lack of drive.

To be successful, penalties must be closely related to the misbehaviour in time.

For teenagers, the threat of not traveling six months from now due to failing a test is unhelpful. Spending additional time studying over the next three days and therefore forfeiting the benefit of afternoon leisure time is a quick and effective solution.

Short-term: My parents grounded me for life when I was 13 years old. To be successful, logical consequences must be relatively short-lived. Once again, this relates to the concept of time.

Anything lasting more than few days or weeks for most teenagers becomes ineffective (as long as the outcome is severe and rapid).

Anything longer generates anger, scorn and vengeance and invalidates any life lessons imparted.

Parenting teenagers is intended to prepare them for life on their own. Using the R's and S's of consequences enables parents to maintain control while imparting life lessons.

Before discussing anger management for children, it's a good idea to examine Webster's dictionary. According to Webster's Dictionary, yell means:

- To make a loud cry, scream or shout. Now, if you're a well-to-do parent who uses yelling as a form of discipline, excuse me while I channel my best Dr. Phil voice ("How's that going for ya?").

One of the most effective strategies for getting your child to behave is to refrain from yelling at them for not tidying their room. Even if you have informed them of the 44th time this month, yelling usually has the opposite impact or you can encounter plain old resistance. Parents pound their heads against the walls, perplexed why young Johnny refuses to cooperate after being shouted at the entire day.

To add insult to injury, yelling parents are taken aback when their child begins to perform the one thing they have observed their youngster do many nights—yell.

Yes, young Johnny's windpipes are capable of delivering poisonous poison and causing pain to unwary parents. He learned from the best, his parents and the absence of effective anger control methods for children.

At the same time, parents may mean well when they scream at their children for breaking the boundaries they create; screaming serves to encourage a youngster to dig their heels in. It is ineffective.

How does a yelling parent improve their anger management skills for children so that a youngster gets the lesson loud and clear?

The first step is to quit yelling and teach your youngster that expected behaviour is the best behaviour for everyone. Rather than shouting at Little Johnny for his untidy room, show him the mis-shapen cookies that have been sitting by his Xbox for four days.

Allow him to smell the strange socks he has been refusing to put in the hamper for weeks. However, what if being clear is ineffective; what if you have a clear, level head and Little Johnny continues to refuse to move?

Maintain your composure and refrain from screaming. Other than that, speak with Little Johnny about his ways. Perhaps he requires your assistance in getting started.

You might promise him that if he keeps his room clean, you'll buy him his favourite Xbox game or you could promise him that if he keeps his room clean, you'll take him to see that Pixar film he's been dying to watch. In other words, make use of the reward system. Many studies have demonstrated that persons who are rewarded respond far more than those who are punished.

Chapter 5

Is Child Anger Management Truly Child's Play?

A teenager's hormones are out of control and having a teenager who appears to be in control constantly is not always a good thing.

As a teenager in the 1970s, it was usual for parents to be harsh with their children. If their child displayed anger in a particular setting, it was assumed that the parent would advise them to "control yourself " or "turn that frown upside-down," as if the youngster could manage the emotion like a faucet.

To compound matters, parents who were fortunate enough to elicit communication from their children would then denigrate them with words like "that's nothing when I was your age."

This is not what a teenager wants to hear, nor is it what a teenager wants to hear now. Understanding why children become upset is one thing; we also need to understand how our teen communicates their anger early in their development.

Some adolescents join violent sports teams or engage in roughhousing with their peers. This allows for the release of aggression in a safe manner when properly supervised but often, in the spirit of competition, adults who should know better channel the teen's aggressive nature and amp it up by giving them steroids or weight loss drugs, which only add to the overstimulated teen mind.

To determine if your child has an anger problem early on, it helps to be familiar with their hobbies and interests. Their music can evolve, as can their artwork, becoming more violent or grim. Nowadays, video games are played by children who channel their frustrations into the game. Keep an eye out for and learn about your teenagers.

Take the time to inquire about their activities in an open-minded manner.

Show real interest in their work.

Avoid becoming a "judgmental parent" who always has a bad opinion about everything they do.

Be there for them when they're ready and you'll be one of the people they turn to for assistance when they're in need.

Never be frightened or too proud to tell your children when they cause you pain.

They can be so preoccupied with getting through their day that they are unaware and we are entering into this talk believing that your teen loves you. It doesn't matter whether they claim they "hate you." Engage in their lives. After they are on their own, you have plenty of time to become the best bowler or dart thrower.

My daughter may initiate many of these "family occasions" with a dilemma over her school grades or perhaps a friend or classmate spread a lie about her to the entire class.

We may even get into a passionate disagreement about how unfair life is but if you are patient and hold to your values while allowing your child time to vent and reflect, they generally come up with their solution, cry, hug you and express their gratitude for your presence.

They retire to bed and you remain awake, wondering what you did that was so significant to them while they continue to struggle with the same issues. However, they feel more confident in their ability to care for themselves. On the other hand, your teenagers do not want you to fight their battles for them; they want to fight them on their own. They become frustrated when they are cannot.

Rest, nutritious food, and exercise are often required to return to life and see if they can make it through another day because it is truly what every parent wants.

Anger management for children is an excellent way to understand better what your child is experiencing or feeling throughout their outbursts. Two significant things can affect a child's behaviour: adult activities and the influence of the media. These innocent children have witnessed some hostility and utilize what they have witnessed to show others incorrect during conflicts.

Influence of Adults

For hours at a time, some children in violent households are exposed to furious adults. They quickly adopt these similar tendencies when they are with other children - arguing and fighting. If the youngster does not attend a session on child anger management, the explosiveness can develop into an issue.

Aggressive adults should be mindful of their behaviour around children since they can impact how they interact with their classmates. If you must argue, please do so in another room or away from the child.

The Media's Influence

Children are maturing faster than ever before due to R-rated films, violent cartoons and crass comedy in the media. Anger management techniques become ineffective when a child has been exposed to more than 3-4 hours of this type of entertainment, as the child will copy what they see.

A child's ability to act out past media scenarios might be a significant issue in elementary schools. Children develop hostile attitudes toward one another, which results in confrontations. Anger management programs for youngsters may help everyone including the adults feel better.

Make It Correct

To address this, anger management for children should begin with a more sensual, in-depth discussion with the child about what upsets them. Understanding these characteristics may assist the youngster in redirecting their energy toward more constructive activities such as reading or athletics.

If taught properly, their habits can be reshaped into more positive, friendlier ones. Children can also learn how to manage their anger in health department seminars or elementary therapy sessions.

Consult your child's school or day-care about enrolling them in one of these classes to help them learn how to manage their anger toward others. All you can do is observe, learn from and listen to what your youngster says. You can discover that some of the things you performed harmed this behaviour.

Chapter 6

Is Childhood Anger a Result of Nature or Nurture?

The percentage of children with severely poor anger management skills and an inability to control their impulses increases. Recent headlines about children murdering other children, perpetrating school shootings and assassinating their parents have led some to speculate that some children are born nasty or are these children solely the product of a substandard family environment?

Are they the result of natural selection, nurture or a combination of the two?

Organic reasons for brain dysfunction may contribute to children's aggressive, furious and destructive behaviour. There is some evidence that extreme stress during pregnancy might increase Another probable explanation for these inclinations is severe physical abuse, which damages the brain's frontal lobes, which assists in impulse and reaction control.

Children become furious when they witness family aggression or when their parents ignore their basic needs. They believe that no one is concerned about them. Excessive stress during their formative years may change their brain chemistry. These mistreated and/or neglected children develop an attitude toward others that views them as things to be used.

Their lack of early socialization and bonding skills develops them into callous adults who believe they are justified in injuring others. They perceive the aggressor in the home to wield absolute power and yearn for similar authority for themselves. As a result, they become aggressive and have no qualms about imposing their will on others.

Some young individuals resort to violence because they perceive no other way to cope with the emotions they are experiencing at the time. They can be unaware of the repercussions of violent action.

It is your responsibility as a parent to assist your child in learning and developing into a responsible member of society. This involves teaching children how to control their anger. After all, everyone becomes furious and life is unjust.

This instruction begins immediately but can be more difficult for some children. I have a three-year-old son who is rather explosive when he is upset. Managing these times will require a lot of effort, resolve and patience on my part. Here are some suggestions on what to do if your youngster becomes furious.

- Remain Calm.

As a parent, you want to avoid spanking or being furious at your child for being upset. They express emotion, and as I have learned, emotions are neither right nor bad. Therefore, if your child is furious, maintain your composure and assist them in expressing their displeasure more suitably.

- Recognize their anger as natural.

After all, everyone becomes furious at times. Due to, your youngster is perfectly normal. They are not wrong or bad for being upset and you are not a poor parent for allowing this to happen to your child.

- Assist them in verbalizing their emotions.

If children can communicate their concerns and be heard by you, they will positively deal with them.

- Attempt to remove them from the situation.

Take them to a different area to speak with them and distract them from their furious feelings. This will aid them in hearing and comprehending you more effectively.

- Teach children to respect boundaries.

Your children must understand that it is acceptable to be unhappy but not acceptable to behave badly due to it. For instance, you could remark, "It is acceptable to be unhappy but it is not acceptable to smack your sister in anger." Keep it concise and straight to the point, as they will forget much of what you are teaching if they are unhappy.

Children typically respond to anger in the same way their families do. As a result, it is your responsibility as a parent to serve as a positive role model for your children. Often, adjusting how you handle situations as an adult can significantly impact how your child manages them.

These strategies may assist you if you believe your child is withdrawing or exploding excessively over minor irritations:

- Evaluate your own ability to handle your anger. Are you a role model for youngsters to emulate?

- Instil fundamental problem-solving skills and the ability to moderate one's anger. When distressing events occur, the youngster who has mastered these abilities is more likely to consider the repercussions and be better equipped to make nonviolent choices.

- Demonstrate confidence in their abilities to acquire effective anger management skills and serve as a role model for positive behaviour.

- Encourage the youngster to take a walk away from sources of stress and spend time engaging in things they enjoy. A change in location or activity can help divert attention away from the source of the anger.

- Explain to your child that everyone has anger, discuss a time when you felt truly furious and discuss healthy strategies to deal with anger.

If none of these strategies work seeks assistance. Consult a physician or paediatrician. You can decide that your child and family require assistance from someone with professional mental health training in developing good anger management skills.

Chapter 7

Where Do The Children Hide?

At home, anger management issues create an unpleasant environment for the entire family. On the other hand, children are often the most harmed by these outbursts, yet the ones who suffer the least attention.

Adults in the hot head's household often counterattack and express their feelings to the furious individual. This often results in both parties being furious, with the children becoming caught in the crossfire.

The bad thing about children is that they are incapable of expressing their emotions. Without a doubt, most children caught in this situation are fearful. They are extremely unlikely to speak up due to this anxiety, extending much beyond the angry outburst.

All too often, people who struggle with anger management have no idea how much harm is being done to these children at the time. Indeed, it is improbable that they see the children getting up and leaving the area where the outburst occurs.

Then, once everything has returned to normal, no concern is given to where the children have gone. Children may withdraw to their rooms or to the backyard to escape the sting and dread of the anger.

Adolescents seek refuge on the street and the establishment of an unhealthy environment becomes a risk. Children loitering on the street to escape the atmosphere at home are not a good situation.

Individuals who struggle with anger management issues must pay close attention to what is going on around them. It is true and acceptable that the individual who suffers from angry outbursts may have no control over the situation.

However, that individual cannot control their empathy for the children and their ability to imagine themselves in their position. Consider how upsetting it must be for children to witness a parent they rely on spiralling out of control. Yet they are aware that decisive action to rectify the situation would be taken if it were them.

Young angry outbursts also send the message to these children that this type of behaviour is acceptable. It should not surprise a parent when their child begins to emulate their emotional outburst acts.

The bottom line is that children should not have to retreat to their rooms, backyards or streets to avoid an unpleasant environment generated by anger management issues. There is no reason for this when so much assistance and support are available to struggling with anger management issues.

Parents must recognize the source of their children's anger and work to resolve it rather than complaining about it. The primary source of anger in most youngsters is their reliance on adults for most of their needs.

This, combined with their inability to articulate their desires and wishes clearly, frustrates them. Also, loneliness is a factor. When children feel as if they require additional attention, they begin shouting and screaming. If anger is not managed effectively, it might escalate into violence.

Here are some recommendations for parents on knowing where your children hide as regards anger.

Distinguish between anger and aggression: Parents must communicate with their children and help them understand that anger is just another emotion. Everybody gets furious from time to time but it must be conveyed in a controlled and non-aggressive manner. As with joy, expressing love does not harm others; similarly, expressing anger should not cause harm to anybody.

Never retaliate or punish: When youngsters are furious, they should not be reprimanded or punished. Other than that, parents must speak softly and demonstrate their love by physical expressions such as hugs and kisses, pats on the back and so on.

This would be reassuring and provide the child with a sense of security. The youngster should be taught gently what is and is not appropriate behaviour and the standards of acceptable behaviour.

Illustrate: Children are constantly attempting to emulate their parents. As a result of this, parents must set an example. They should refrain from screaming or yelling when they are anxious. Other than that, they employ anger control strategies.

Along with reassuring children of parental support, parents must also educate them on managing their anger. The following are some suggestions for managing one's anger.

To calm the youngster and distract his attention, instruct them to take a deep breath and count from 1 to 10 and from 10 to 1.

Instruct the youngster to jump, touch his nose and so forth to draw out negative energy. If nothing else is practicable, instruct the youngster to seek adult assistance quickly.

Engaging children in creative activities such as dance, music and art teaches them how to express their emotions constructively.

Participating in physical activities such as riding, walking, and swimming teaches youngsters how to positively manage their anger.

Rewarding youngsters for excellent behaviour encourages positive behaviour and discourages aggressiveness.

Yoga and meditation are excellent ways to channel energy in a constructive direction.

A change in environment would assist the child in regaining his composure. Physically relocating the youngster would be beneficial.

Discussing with the child how you handled a similar circumstance in a controlled manner will assist the child in calming down.

The above management methods will undoubtedly assist children in regaining control of their tempers. They are most effective if they are adopted before the child reaches the age of seven. Also, it is vital to comprehend the source of the anger and treat the issue to achieve a lasting resolution.

Chapter 8

Are You Fighting a Lost Fight as a parent? What Are Your Intentions?

This may come as no surprise, but anger management for children typically begins with the child's normal development. While anger can be a phase that youngsters go through, if it is not reined in by parents who are positive role models for their children, it can develop into an uncontrollable two-headed monster.

If not checked during a child's tween years, parents should brace themselves for all-out conflict as tweens enter their early teen years. Thus, while it is generally recommended to nip it in the bud while children are still young, parents often struggle to regain control of a disruptive child.

To regain control of a disruptive child and hone your anger management skills for children, a responsible parent requires a plan. The plan's purpose should be one and only one thing: respect.

When a child demonstrates respect for their parent(s), they are less likely to exhibit an aggressive, confrontational attitude. Daily training should be included in a parent's strategy, as it will take time to establish new learned habits. Not only will a parent have to change their child's attitude, but they may discover that their views need to be changed as well.

Parents attempting to instil a new attitude in their children should first pose the following question to themselves in front of a mirror. How can I begin by changing myself?

This generally begins with a parent letting rid of any selfish characteristics. Many parents will go insane if their child disobeys, which encourages them to react against the parent. Remember that a child is a child.

They will make mistakes, but it is up to you as a parent to gently explain that the error was an error. If you find yourself yelling at your child for making a mistake, you are not teaching; you are merely adding salt to an open sore.

Children's anger control begins with a deliberate, calm, harmonic and low-key approach. Parents must plan for how they will deal with a disruptive youngster. Parents should consider their response if something goes wrong.

This will avoid any unwanted spontaneous anger on the parent's part and in response, children will have greater respect for their parents. While planning, remember that children will be children, which includes some naughty behaviour. They should not be chastised for spilling milk on the floor or grabbing M&M's at the neighbourhood grocery store.

Would you yell at a tiger only because he had strips?

A youngster may not always possess the maturity to be optimistic in all circumstances. It is not a simple task to grow up in today's culture, which often results in teenagers being forced to be shifty.

Teenagers, on the whole, are not considerate individuals. They are constantly in competition and distrust plays a significant role in their behaviour. The constant rat race to the top is pervasive in the adolescent world. This is unfortunate and upsetting, as these are supposed to be their greatest years.

Nowadays, teenagers are expected to mature well before their time, continuously confronted with obstacles. While some of them are capable of dealing with it, others tend to construct a defensive wall. When confronted with difficulty, many teenagers exhibit negative behaviours; some even become irresponsible, even to the point of violence or, in severe circumstances, death.

Adopting anger management tactics in adolescents can be a Herculean endeavour, as they often refuse to follow the advice and are rarely willing to follow directions.

To create a successful anger management program, create something that focuses on the necessary flaws without being overbearing. One of the most difficult problems is persuading adolescent children that they have behavioural concerns. Nevertheless, it is a necessary task.

If anger is not managed, it has the potential to take over a person's life, wreaking havoc on not just his progress but also on all other aspects of his existence. When teenagers are angry, their default response is yelling and screaming; they often wind up saying terrible things, punching walls, damaging items, shoving other people around and even injuring themselves.

Although it may appear unattainable, it is important that they are convinced and encouraged to learn anger management strategies for their well-being and the well-being of others around them.

Teens can positively improve their lives with excellent anger management skills, which will result in success, prosperity and happiness. The appropriate anger management training should teach children to be self-aware, to evaluate their emotions to determine the source of their anger.

They should work on self-control, i.e., pause and consider their reactions even when upset; this will help avoid unintended consequences. They should be taught to make judgments not in the heat of the moment but after deliberating over the many options and weighing the consequences.

This envisioned scenario is then studied and compared to what would have transpired if they had acted on impulse. This enables children to comprehend the gravity of their acts. If used consistently, this strategy will eventually become ingrained in their system and making deliberate choices will become second nature to the teens.

Like any other age group, teenagers have their minds, preferences, and dislikes, but they can be overly enthusiastic about their positions at times. This can be due to hormones, but it does not change the fact that it occasionally complicates matters.

Teens can benefit greatly from exercise, sports, listening to music and maintaining a diary. The most effective strategy to assist people in controlling their anger is to tailor an anger management program to their preferences and choices.

If the child's anger becomes unmanageable, their guardians or the teens themselves may seek professional aid. Most would agree that a skilled hypnotherapist can be of tremendous assistance in this endeavour.

Chapter 9

When Is It Ideal for a Parent to Be Concerned?

Children's anger management is not something to take lightly. Indeed, it is one of the most important aspects of child-rearing that most parents should strive to excel in before their children enter their teen and adolescent years.

However, if you haven't mastered the art of raising naughty children and are concerned about whether your child's behaviour warrants professional intervention, there are a few symptoms to look for.

If your child occasionally throws a tantrum when they do not get their way, this is not a warning for a parent to be concerned that professional therapy is required. Children are naturally interested and curiosity can lead to bad behaviour.

You should not be too irritated if your toddler goes into the cabinet and spills a 5-pound bag of sugar on your table. In this case, yelling at a youngster is pointless; this child requires explaining why not spill sugar.

Suppose your youngster exhibits hostility in the presence of other children. While this may not be the reason for alarm, children can become envious if they believe someone is attempting to "take" their mother or father. Small occurrences like this are a natural part of a child's development; these difficult times in a child's life will pass quickly.

When is it appropriate for a parent to be concerned about their child's behaviour?

When should a parent seek professional assistance with child anger management?

That is not a subject that can be answered in a single chapter because every situation and child is unique, but some indicators may raise some red flags for concerned parents. Is your youngster physically abusive or hurls objects at other people?

If it occurs once or twice, you should not be frightened; but, if this violence becomes a part of your child's daily life, it can be time to see a professional counsellor. Is your youngster verbally abusing siblings and/or friends? Parents should not take this aspect of child anger management lightly; if parents allow children to get away with it, violent verbal attacks will only worsen.

Do your child's temper tantrums endure an extended amount of time?

There should be no cause for alarm if your child is upset for a few minutes because you refuse to let them watch their favourite Shrek movie. Still, if the behaviour persists for hours and your child becomes physically aggressive, you should seek more assistance. If parenting children is the most difficult job in the world, raising aggressive children is the most difficult job in the Universe.

As this is a potentially explosive situation, parents should understand the difference between normal and aggressive behaviour. If you're still undecided between the two, do nothing. Please consult an expert because it is preferable to state that you are unsure and refrain from doing than to be incorrect and act with malice.

Effective parenting requires children to control their anger. Let's examine this scenario:

Little Johnny enters Walmart's hair salon. He looks adorable in his Yankees hat and Buster Brown sneakers. I knew he was three years old because he kept holding up four fingers and shouting to everyone within hearing distance that he was three years old. I immediately forgot about Little Johnny's cuteness as he began to reveal his true colours.

Johnny dashed to the first empty stylist chair he spotted. As he ascended, he twirled around on the chair, screaming "Yippee. He then grabbed a hot curling iron that was fortunately not on. Little Johnny's mother gently explained, "Johnny, if you don't behave, Santa won't visit you this Christmas."

That is the issue.

The primary cause of inadequate anger control in youngsters is a failure to be strict when necessary. Parents often allow children to misbehave for an extended period before summoning the guts to say what should have been spoken minutes earlier—returning to Little Johnny.

His mother should have established the ground rules before he entered the salon. She should have reprimanded him immediately for leaping into the chair. She let many incidences pass before partially correcting his naughty habits. Three lessons that any well-off parent can implement into their child-raising discipline practices are as follows:

1. Do not allow youngsters to commit multiple crimes before intervening. "You must nip it in the bud," Andy Griffith would say.

2. If your child does disobey you, disregard their methods of gaining attention. (weeping, moaning)

3. Be unambiguous (Let your child know what you expect, leave no ambiguity)

According to recent studies, (carried out by the Child Mind Institute) anger management for children works best when the youngster has a strong understanding of the risk/reward relationship. If Little Johnny understands that throwing a hair spray can elicit an unfavourable response from his mother, he will reconsider his conduct.

If he understands that spinning in the salon chair will very certainly result in him missing out on a Happy Meal, he will sit there like the perfect angel as Happy Meal boxes dance about in his head.

If you are a parent who has negatively influenced your child's conduct, implementing these lessons will provide parents an advantage in their relationship with their children. After all, what child will risk losing a Happy Meal by spinning in a chair?

There are not many.

Chapter 10

Does Your Obstinate, Out-Of-Control Child Have Control Issues?

If you often find yourself in power battles with your adolescent as a parent, the following developmental phases may help you understand why:

The child believes in stage 1 that "I am in control only when I am noticed or served."

Generally, if the parent provides opportunities for positive attention, the problem does not worsen. If the parent does not provide opportunities for positive attention, the youngster will seek it through inappropriate behaviour (negative attention).

Suppose the parent succumbs to the negative attention OR becomes furious and punishes the child for seeking negative attention. In that case, the youngster may temporarily stop acting out but quickly resumes the acting-out behaviour and progresses to stage 2.

At stage 2, the child believes that "I am in charge only when I am the boss or am demonstrating that no one can boss me."

When a parent withdraws from a power struggle, establishes firm boundaries and acts without becoming angry, the problem usually does not worsen. If the parent allow a child to be the boss OR retaliates in anger, the child's disobedience persists and worsens - and the child progresses to stage 3.

At stage 3, the youngster believes: "I am in charge only when I cause harm to others."

If the parent establishes clear boundaries and does not take the attacks personally, the condition does not deteriorate significantly. If the parent gives in, surrenders or lashes out at the child in anger, the child's misbehaviour continues and increases - and the child may progress to stage 4.

At stage 4, the child believes: "I am in control solely by convincing others that they should not expect anything from me. I am incapable. I am powerless."

If the parent quits up and accepts the child's perspective of helplessness, weakness and inability, the child's condition will persist.

Act "as if " you are not angry, as a parent! When our child is furious and we react angrily to their anger, anger is multiplied by two. It's the equivalent of attempting to extinguish a fire with a flamethrower rather than a water hose - it only makes matters worse. As difficult as it can be, we must maintain a poker face in response to our child's anger - show no emotion!

When we respond to our child's anger with additional anger, we may convince the youngster to behave temporarily. Still, when the next problem arises, the child's anger will be even greater.

Then we are engaged in a power battle (in other words, his anger is at level 5 .we respond at level 5 .the next time, his anger is at level 6 .we respond with a 6 .the next time his anger is at level 7 .we respond with 7 .and so on).

If the parent gives in OR lashes out in anger in reaction to the child's actions (passive response vs. aggressive response), the child becomes increasingly furious. This is how it works:

1st - Child wishes to thwart you; forgets to do what you ask; plays dumb; expresses displeasure by what he does not do; often whines and moans.

If you, as the parent, respond quietly or angrily – or both – he progresses to the next level of anger.

2nd - The child ignores you and treats you silently.

If you react passively or violently, he progresses to the next stage of anger.

3rd - He believes something is wrong with you and informs you; he wants you to feel bad because he is angry; he informs you that it is your responsibility.

If you react passively or violently, he progresses to the next stage of anger.

4th - He uses profanity, yells, shouts.

If you react passively or violently, he progresses to the next stage of anger.

5th - He makes statements such as "It's going to go my way or else I'm fleeing."

I'm going to demolish the house while you're at work" " I'm going to move in with my father." "I'm going to quit school" etc.

If you react passively or violently, he progresses to the next stage of anger.

6th - This is where physical violence enters the scene. This violence can be somewhat averted if the child is aware of what he is doing, even if he subsequently claims it was an accident. The child intends to stop once he has his desired outcome. If the adult yields, he will back off.

During this final stage, property destruction and domestic battery may occur, the cops can be called (sometimes by the child), the parent may file an incorrigibility charge, the child can be unaware of his behaviour, can become suicidal or may physically harm the parent.

To end power disputes, it must be the parent who takes a constructive leadership role. An effective course of action is to cease debating. It sounds simple: stop arguing but it requires a lot of discipline and work to do so.

If the parent refuses to engage in the debates, the out-of-control child's power evaporates. If you refuse to get drawn into a power struggle, the disagreement devolves into a temper tantrum.

Chapter 11

How Can Anger Management Assist in Coping With Adolescent Behaviour Issues?

Teenage behaviour problems might be aggravated if you, as a parent, become furious about trivial matters. Anger management for parents is important if you want to resolve some of your children's behavioural challenges. Finally, you must recognize that your adolescent is a product of you.

If you haven't learned to control your anger and have been unreasonable throughout your life, you cannot expect your child to grow up to be a sensible, well-behaved adolescent. As a result, if you wish to deal with teenage behavioural issues, you must first learn to control your anger.

There are communication improvement models that can assist parents in structuring difficult conversations with their children.

The model is followed by a working activity that will assist you in practicing the model and considering all possible outcomes before having the conversation to obtain an effective result. However, it all begins with your capacity to control your emotions and the following are some strategies for dealing with severe adolescent behaviour issues:

1. Ignore minor hiccups: Avoid many anger-inducing situations. You must concentrate on truly serious behavioural issues rather than becoming irritated with non-harmful behaviour.

   This means that the day you take their acts seriously and examine their behaviour with them, they will understand that what they have done is not insignificant and that they owe you an explanation. Ignoring minor setbacks is important for effective anger management.

2. Another effective method of managing anger is to neutralize prospective conflicts before they escalate into a fight; If you know that you will have a dispute with your teenager every morning because they will skip breakfast or wear what you consider to be unsuitable clothing, try ignoring the annoying behaviour for a while, depriving it of its significance.

3. If the teenager is hungry, they will eat later and if you make no comment and choose to wear warm clothing on a cold day, they will do so without feeling defeated.

4. Understand your parenting partner; the parent who begins dealing with the teenager's bad behaviour sees it through to the conclusion, unless the parent becomes furious, at which point the parent takes a time-out and the other parent, who is typically much calmer, steps in.

This teaches your adolescent that the calmer you are, the more equipped you can solve an issue. Getting assistance from a close relative, such as your spouse, is the best course of action for anger control.

5. Counting is a highly effective method of managing anger. Count backward from ten. Count aloud so that your adolescent may hear you. When they inquire as to why you're counting, you might explain that it assists you in remaining cool before being furious, as you don't want to yell at them or lose control.

6. Inform them that they, too, may try it. Being a role model is the most effective strategy to address teenage behaviour issues associated with disruptive behaviour.

7. Apologize to your teenager if you do blow up; you are only human after all. By apologizing for being abrupt, furious or yelling and screaming at them, they will realize that if we lose control, we will apologize later, as this is not acceptable behaviour.

Mom became furious and yelled at me but afterward apologized: she still loves me despite her outburst. You can truly master all the anger mentioned above management techniques if you learn to set your ego aside and apologize when you make a mistake.

Teenagers are often in a state of bewilderment as they approach their teens and it is this misunderstanding causes them to behave inappropriately.

Recognizing their stage of life and providing unwavering support is important in navigating this era of their lives. You can create the proper balance in your family and avoid unneeded distractions by utilizing the many anger management strategies described above.

(This page is intentionally blank)

Chapter 12

What To Do When Things Get Out Of Hand

Children are not always forthcoming with their sentiments and emotions. Thoughts of anguish and guilt can plague a child but it is improbable that you will discover this during a conversation.

A child's behaviour often reflects his emotions. When a child is upset, he will likely isolate himself and have little to say. When he is guilty, he avoids human contact and retreats to his room.

When a youngster needs anger management, they will destroy their toys, yell and/or throw tantrums. Children are not usually outspoken about their emotions but their actions will speak for them if their words do not.

When children demonstrate anger through outbursts and tossing themselves about on the floor in tantrums, they must go through the process of learning what anger management for children may teach them. These actions serve as indicators to a parent that their child requires assistance. If left handled, this issue could grow into a sea of future difficulties.

Anger management is offered for these youngsters and is useful in resolving their issues with anger. Finding the greatest resources for children's anger control requires research and experimentation. Many resources exist that offer advice on how to handle your child's anger.

Assisting a youngster in managing his emotions may need the use of child-specific programs. A youngster will not benefit from attending an adult anger group or enrol in an anger management course.

While these guidelines are wonderful for adults, they are inappropriate for children. Their minds have not yet grown sufficiently for them to be able to communicate their emotions to others. In all honesty, they can be unaware of what is occurring.

A counsellor does not expect a youngster to open up and express the precise emotions that cause him to be angry. These details are obtained through different activities designed to teach children about anger management.

Children respond strongly to action activities, so incorporating games into their therapy will effectively teach children about anger management. Children should learn positive values and acceptable behaviour through games rather than attending a one-on-one counselling session.

When worksheets, colouring books, quizzes and puzzles are included, anger management for children becomes instantly exciting and fun. At these times, children can be engaged in a program without being aware of it.

To small children, anger management is a challenging concept to grasp. Given that youngsters are uninformed of their precise emotions and cannot think rapidly and analyse their choices, it is exceedingly difficult to teach children effective lesson plans that demand logical thinking.

Children need to learn how to moderate their anger. A child must learn how to behave appropriately in different scenarios. They must understand that while it is entirely acceptable to be furious, they must equally understand that this anger should not be abused.

Teaching youngsters early on how to control their anger will provide the groundwork for their future. Through repetition of activities and practices, children gradually develop an understanding of anger management for children.

Working with them and utilizing constructive tactics can significantly assist the child's upbringing. Anger can result in irrational behaviour and decisions and it is in the best interests of both parents and children to address the issue as soon as feasible. That is why it is vital to teaching your child how to manage unpleasant emotions appropriately from an early age.

The sooner you can teach your child appropriate strategies to deal with anger, the sooner your child will be able to confront the many natural stresses of childhood, particularly the tumultuous teen years, with confidence and optimism. The following are some tips to assist you and your children in dealing with anger issues.

It is crucial to maintain your composure during abrupt outbursts and be tough and consistent in enforcing discipline so that your child takes you seriously. You want your child to feel a little better about himself for being upset and that there are better ways to deal with it. You do not want to contribute to or feed into a child's anger by becoming irritable and exploding with anger.

Also, you can need to discuss appropriate methods of expressing discontent or anger, such as avoiding specific situations, gently requesting replacements or coaching on other ways to do something.

Allow your children to understand in plain language which actions may not be permitted by society's norms, such as uncontrolled speaking and yelling profanity, throwing items and tantrums, slamming doors and yelling in public or refusing to participate in family duties or homework.

When was the last time your child expressed their anger?

What was your reaction?

Are you aware of why your child became so furious?

These are just a few of the questions you might consider if you notice that your child is constantly irritable. Be emphatic and attempt to understand why the child is irritable, what is truly causing those feelings and assist them from that perspective.

Parents may employ various constructive strategies to establish a strong relationship with their children, control their anger, and even better, redirect their anger toward more productive channels.

Because each child is unique and household circumstances vary significantly, one thing may not apply universally. I hope this encourages you to be patient and educate your loved ones on how to deal with annoyance and feelings of anger most positively and healthily possible.

Chapter 13

How to Handle Adolescent Anger Effectively

The adolescent years are important for a child's development. Regrettably, these are the years during which children confront some of their most difficult situations.

This precise period in a child's life can affect them differently, not all of them pleasant. Teen children who are forced to live in traumatic situations often lash out. Many teen children develop a risky attitude. When adolescents experience angry emotions and begin to act out, it can be time to seek help for their children.

Toddlers, particularly young children, are typically unaware of their feelings. When a child is disturbed or angry, they express their feelings through their conduct. A good illustration of this is the small child who throws a tantrum because he is upset.

Many senior citizens have encountered similar circumstances. Regrettably, these instances are often disregarded or dismissed as "children." Anger control in children is just as important, if not more so than anger management in adults.

From the time a child is born until they reach adulthood, they require training and guidance. The lessons they absorb throughout their childhoods are likely to shape who they become as adults. Due to, youngsters who have difficulty controlling their temper are important. Finding techniques to demonstrate anger management to children could provide difficulties.

Young children can benefit from worksheets, games and enjoyable activities. Possibly the best course of action would be to develop programs that integrate all these. When a youngster is doing a worksheet, colouring page or participating in games and activities with underlying messages about anger control, they can be unaware they are addressing their issue.

Making the activity enjoyable does not imply that the anger issue must be ignored. Choosing enjoyable activities that promote healthy interaction and decision-making can be wise for children's anger management.

Teach children to take turns and to understand that they cannot always be the best or the winner will positively differentiate them in aggressive circumstances. Very few activities that promote morals and encourage good thinking might benefit your youngster.

When confronted with a highly charged scenario, self-awareness and self-management go hand in hand. Anger management for children encourages the youngster to analyse their emotions, possessions and the true source of the conflict. Taking a few seconds to meditate on these concepts in their mind may affect their action or reaction.

While dealing with adolescents who have anger issues can be difficult, there are many resources accessible. The Internet is an excellent source of information on this subject. While teaching anger control strategies is not easy, the results are well worth the effort. If the challenge prevents a youngster from experiencing harm or pain, it is unquestionably worthwhile.

The parental focus must unquestionably be anger control for children. If children aren't taught how to control their anger throughout their formative years, they may encounter serious challenges as adults.

As a result, it becomes an important role of parents to assist their children in developing the ability to handle unpleasant emotions appropriately from an early age. Even toddlers can benefit from a rudimentary understanding of anger control, despite the certainty that tantrums will occur occasionally.

According to Columbia University College of Physicians and Surgeons and the New York State Psychiatric Institute, most child behaviour problems reflect what they have witnessed throughout their formative years.

These might include adult partner violence, such as severe punishment and the child being exposed to abusive interactions between parents and other adults.

The next few chapters will discuss some anger management ideas that will assist you in dealing with child anger management.

(This page is intentionally blank)

Chapter 14

Addressing Children's Anger Management in Novel Ways

While it's natural to lose patience when dealing with a very rebellious or furious youngster, you're supporting the child's hostile behaviour by doing so. Instead of reacting with anger, you might use some playful methods to help the youngster recognize the excessive nature of their anger.

Although this can be difficult in very hot situations, the quicker you get the youngster to express their emotions, the more quickly you can calm the situation and talk efficiently. In comparison to adult anger management, child anger management is less limiting. It is feasible to utilize more inventive tactics with children.

The first step is to call attention to the obvious.

If your youngster is acting abnormally furious, calmly point this out. You should not tease your youngster about it but rather demonstrate to them the folly of raving and ranting. Pretend their remarks are blowing you over or respond with an exaggerated expression of surprise. Keep your message brief but your response light-hearted.

Because children lack the social experience that adults do, they cannot pick up on subtle nuances. Therefore, you do not need to be delicate while discussing anger management for children. If their anger does not destroy yours, you will be able to dismantle the child's emotional fortifications.

The second stage is to create space.

If the child continues to ignore your attempts despite your light-hearted and calm response, there is no harm in expressing your unwillingness to deal with the child in their angry mood and walking away.

If the child follows you shouting after you use this strategy, calmly remind them that you can speak with them only when they have calmed down and that you will not react to them until their anger has dissipated.

You'll know whether you've successfully communicated your message if the child understands that they must overcome their anger to gain your attention. If your message is constant, the child will quickly learn how to manage their anger.

If you recall how frustrating it was to be a youngster and to want to be heard, you will have the key to effective child anger management. In anger management for children, it is less a symptom of underdevelopment than in adults and more of an unlearned lesson. The best professors are not always the most rigid.

When dealing with anger management for children, remember that the best teachers can look past the child's outward reaction to the small child within who is pleading for assistance.

Parents reading this are unlikely to be startled by recent findings from a team of researchers at the University of Georgia School of Medicine. The study, which is the first of its kind and was published in the November issue of Paediatric Exercise Science, a professional journal dedicated to advancing our understanding of exercise in childhood, discovers that aerobic activity appears to affect children's anger management significantly.

Indeed, aerobic exercise can be a useful technique for assisting overweight children (and possibly children of any weight) in safely, healthfully and rather effectively expelling anger or hostility. An earlier study has demonstrated that exercise can assist children in overcoming depression or anxiety. We have long recognized that exercise can also help older adults manage stress and burn off negative emotions.

The most recent research examined a structured aerobic exercise program on anger expression in healthy overweight children. The researchers examined 208 typically sedentary 7 to 11 year-olds who participated in a 10-15 week after-school aerobics program.

Overweight but healthy participants were randomly allocated to an aerobic exercise program or encouraged to continue their usual inactive routine. At the start and end of the testing, surveys on anger expression were conducted using the Paediatric Anger Expression Scale, which assesses common displays of anger such as slamming doors and striking.

After the testing session, the researchers discovered that the aerobic exercise group had lower Anger-Out and Anger Expression scores. "Exercise had a considerable effect on children's anger expression," Dr. Catherine Davis, a clinical health psychologist at the Medical College of Georgia School of Medicine, explained. "This finding suggests that aerobic exercise can be a useful therapy for overweight children to minimize aggressive behaviour and anger expression."

The finding holds regardless of gender, colour, socioeconomic status or fitness level. This provides another reason for parents, caregivers and educators to encourage children active. Regular exercise appears to benefit not only weight and anger management but also cognitive and insulin resistance.

This latest research confirms Dr. Davis' past findings that aerobic exercise improves cognitive abilities and decreases insulin resistance, a condition considered a precursor to diabetes. While the increased activity helped the study subjects lose weight, they were all still classed as obese after the trial.

Dr. Davis uses a $3.6 million five-year grant from the National Heart, Lung and Blood Institute to determine whether this exercise finding holds for a similar group of children being examined for exercise's effect on cognition.

The scientists want to be some that the improvement in anger scores was caused by exercise and not by other factors such as involvement in a special after-school problem. Changes in daily routines, time spent with parents and away from fight-inducing siblings, violent television and video games may have had a beneficial effect on children's anger control.

Chapter 15

How to get Low-Cost Anger Therapy for Children

Children and teens say the most bizarre things. It makes no difference what they believe or feel; children are not bashful about communicating their emotions with others. While anger management is not always an easy skill for children to acquire, they must do it. Children lack patience but they are quick learners.

The issue is that children do not always express their emotions in predictable or understandable ways.

When a youngster is happy, we can tell by how they interact with their environment: they play, grin and laugh, and are a joy to be around.

Why would we expect them to act differently when they are angry? Why are we as parents so perplexed by children's anger management?

An angry youngster will often act out in socially inappropriate ways, such as throwing tantrums, initiating fights with other children, refusing to cooperate with another child or an adult or speaking back.

When this behaviour occurs, we as parents are often taken aback and fail to recognize it for what it is. We are not always aware of the necessity to intervene and teach our children HOW to manage their anger.

When questioned, children very rarely communicate their sentiments accurately or entirely. When indicators of anger manifest as fits of anger or tantrums, it is important to address the situation immediately. Whatever triggered the child's anger, the issue is the same: anger management.

When children do not learn to manage their anger effectively, it harms their lives - they may have fewer friends and feel excluded. Regrettably, as with everything else with children, what works for one child may not affect another. You may need to experiment to determine the most effective way to assist them in managing their anger.

Friends, family members and other parents can all serve as excellent sources of inspiration. If you are having problems resolving your child's anger, be careful to exhaust all available resources. A fantastic idea can be just around the corner.

Teaching a child to control their anger is just as important as teaching them to walk and talk. There is no way to control the world around us or the behaviour of others but we can manage ourselves and how we engage with it. Self-control enables us to earn the respect of others and ourselves.

A youngster throwing a tantrum is the simplest manifestation of anger. Recognize this display soon and address anger and proper methods of expression with your child to help them understand that there are many ways to express our feelings. Discuss viable alternatives to the current conduct.

Anger difficulties in children are quite problematic, especially when they are still learning about things and unsure what they are dealing with. This is why, as a parent, you have a significant responsibility to assist your child in managing the situation and navigating it successfully.

However, not every parent is aware that their children may have anger issues. This can be quite dangerous since the disease can quickly deteriorate and begin to negatively impact your child's childhood, possibly leading to him being labelled as a problem child.

And because no parent wants their child to go through all of that turmoil, drama and even trauma, it's best if you take the necessary, if not all, precautions to guarantee that your child successfully navigates this phase.

Regrettably, most paediatric therapies are notoriously expensive. However, this should not prevent you from attempting to assist your child. Especially nowadays, with the internet, everything is already at your fingertips, including affordable anger therapy for children.

Due to substantial research on children's health, there are now different strategies you can use to assist your child in managing their anger. Many notable instances that you can find useful include the following:

1. Art therapy for anger. You can assist your youngster in expressing their emotions through the use of art. All you need is some experience administering such activities. Now, you need not worry about where to acquire such assistance, as you can always locate a decent one online, for free or for a modest fee.

2. Anger management therapy for children through the use of games. Games and children have a long-standing positive relationship, making them a great approach for assisting children in managing their anger.

Now, the rules for such games are fairly straightforward. You can play just about any game that occurs to you, but always remember that the primary objective is to calm the children, allowing them to open up more easily to talk to them about their thoughts. By using the game as a springboard for discussion, you can now gain a greater understanding of how your child feels and experiences.

Apart from these two, there are many additional options to obtain low-cost and affordable anger therapy for children. Remember that the goal here is to encourage them to fully express their emotions to reach out to them and reassure them that even though they are experiencing such negativity, everything will be OK and they have nothing to fear.

Teach Them to Visit a Place in Which There Is No Anger

Anger management for children can be a barrier for both children and parents but remember that barriers are not roadblocks; they can be hopped over. Overcoming the hurdle of child anger management requires logic, yet the one thing that logic does not mix well with is emotion.

Because the parent is the rational half of the parent/child duo, it is up to the parent to think logically about reaching their child's emotional side to learn to let go of bottled-up anger on their own.

Many possibilities arise but one is to expose your mischievous child to their sanctuary.

Their sanctuary is filled with all the amazing things they can imagine: a chocolate river with waves formed of warm flowing marshmallows, a candy-striped tree with gummy bear leaves and nestle crunch bar sidewalks.

Children can learn anger management by being taught to go to their sanctuary when they first experience anger, expecting that the anger will decrease and give way to more joyful, heart-warming sentiments.

To begin, this "game" (young children must learn to think in terms of "games") should be played daily for approximately 3-4 minutes due to young children's short attention spans.

After a month, it will become habitual and the youngster will begin visiting their sanctuary whenever they feel bad or undesired emotions. Will having a relaxing tranquil spot to visit mentally put an end to all naughty actions displayed by children? No, but it will reduce the frequency of such unfavourable moments.

Parents must recognize that children will always be children while providing children with options for dealing with their anger management. By their very nature, children may exhibit improper actions from time to time.

You should not be offended by this; after all, would you be offended by an elephant's long tusks?

When a youngster is disruptive, the best thing a parent can do is to demonstrate composure as they observe everything you do. Everything!

Children who struggle with anger often fail to recognize that they have a problem. This is something that the parents must take care of. An effective strategy can be to teach children how to moderate their anger.

The following are some methods in which parents can assist their children in coping with anger:

1. Communicate with youngsters to ascertain their feelings. Take caution not to blame them or convince them that they are bad for experiencing natural anger.

2. Remain with children as they deal with their anger. This teaches children that they are loved regardless of their actions and diminishes the reason for the anger.

3. Assist children incorrectly in expressing their anger. "I loathe this about my friend" is always preferable to "I despise my friend."

4. Prevent youngsters from developing anger. Allow children outlets for their emotions and energies, such as set periods for strenuous physical activity such as football.

5. Set an example for youngsters by controlling your anger and expressing it appropriately.

The following activities can assist youngsters in managing their anger:

1. Enrol your child in a support group for youngsters that offer group anger control activities. This is beneficial for

youngsters who have a tough time communicating their emotions to their parents.

2. Punching a punching bag effectively relieves anger.

3. Children can also benefit greatly from drawing.

Chapter 16

Put An End To False Threats And Promises Immediately!

Your child is adorable. All of your friends adore and admire her for everything she does: the adorable way she says MoMA, the way she eats her string peas and the delightful way she counts to fifteen.

However, there is one detail about your precious little pride and pleasure that your pals are unaware of. She has a reputation for being a tremendous pain in the buttocks. That's true; while your pals are away or when they are present, your child can present a significant challenge to your anger management for children skills.

It typically begins the same way. Parents will note that their toddlers begin expressing anger and violence by striking others or by yelling when they do not get their way. Because children are adorable and little, many parents overlook this behaviour as "temporary."

Parents are horrified to see that the behaviour is not "passing" but is getting worse over time. Unchecked behaviour can easily develop into biting and while biting is a natural part of a toddler's development. They immediately discover that biting is painful and can be used to cause pain.

Last week, I witnessed a youngster bite his mother's arm after she requested he stop playing in the shopping cart. What did she do? She made fabricated threats and assurances about what she would do if her child bit her again.

As far as I can determine, the threats were fabricated and most likely repeated many times throughout the day. I arrived at this conclusion based on her son's behaviour, which indicated that he had heard the identical sentences an endless number of times.

That is the root of the problem when it comes to children's anger management. False threats and promises fall on deaf ears when a youngster has heard the phrase "If you don't stop, I'm going to spank your rear end" 33 times before a parent follows through on these threats. Children can be diminutive in stature but they are mighty in intellect. They discover that momma's warnings are illusory and hence capitalize on this confusing conduct.

Thus, how does a parent reprimand these undesirable attitudes? They can begin by ceasing to speak; parents should concentrate on what they say and recognize the power of their words. Parents must develop the ability to plan what they want to say, how they want to say it and how often they want to say it. Children should understand that when mommy threatens to take away their favourite toy, she means it.

Although it appears as though you have reached a stalemate with your youngster, recognize that other options exist. This technique has endowed me with control over the circumstance. It has taught me to maintain my composure and first to find peace with myself.

Consider the following:

You're at the supermarket, gathering ingredients for tonight's dinner party. When the babysitter cancels at the final minute, Little Johnny is forced to tag along with you as you run errands. Little Johnny experiences a nuclear warhead meltdown in aisle three due to his inability to open the gummy bears.

You put on the most serious expression you can and instantly begin yelling at Johnny for having a temper tantrum over gummy bears as tears stream down his swollen, red cheeks. Every day, youngsters learn anger management lessons in circumstances like this.

Fast forward a few hours, and you and Little Johnny find yourself at Walmart searching for a few birthday favours. Little Johnny, still with dried tears streaks down his cheeks, decides to outdo himself by throwing lettuce at the Walmart clerk and why is that?

Since you did not allow him to ride the bicycles in the aisle, frustrated and furious, you decide to undo Little Johnny's training pants to demonstrate who is boss. You decide to give Little Johnny a hearty embrace after turning his buttocks crimson.

After all, the guilt you're experiencing due to having to spank Johnny is unbearable. Little Johnny is now perplexed; he is aware that he has just committed a wrong but he is now loved and cajoled. Little Johnny is most likely 6 to 8 hours away from his next tirade if he does not receive a clear message.

This is a scene that often occurs in many houses. After raising my children and realized that I needed to brush up on my anger management skills for children, this question troubled me. How much physical discomfort should I inflict on my out-of-control child?

Later, I concluded the answer was none or very little corporal punishment for acts that may result in the death of Little Johnny (running in the street or playing with lighters). While breaking some regulations, such as those described previously, may warrant a few taps on the buttocks, spankings should not be the norm. What, then, will elicit a response from your child?

Sternness: A child will obey a parent who is genuine in their expectations. If a child hears you threaten to punish them for the fourth time today, they will put you to the test to determine your level of commitment to not cleaning their room. They will put you to the test to determine your commitment to moaning about candy at the supermarket.

Allow for some wiggle room and don't be surprised if Little Johnny has a fit because you didn't get him his favourite McDonald's toy. Take your desires seriously. Address your child directly, stating the behaviour you anticipate from them. Before you get in the car, inform them that you will be purchasing only the party goodies you require.

Now that you understand that effective anger management for children requires firm but loving parenting, do you believe that being firm and serious about your expectations will result in Little Johnny being the perfect child? No. Little Johnny will still demonstrate his cunning side; after all, he is a child, especially if the issue has recurred.

If he does experience another meltdown, the best course of action for a parent in this case is to ignore it. Keep a close eye on Little Johnny as he sobs, bites, pulls his hair and moves erratically like a fish on dry land. Ignoring the issue will confound Johnny, as he will learn that his previous methods are ineffective.

Although it appears as though you have reached a stalemate with your youngster, recognize that there is an alternate path to victory. This technique has endowed me with control over the circumstance. It has taught me to maintain my composure and first to find peace with myself.

Chapter 17

The Fail-Proof Strategy for Getting Them to Do What You Request

Many parents will unwillingly confess that they need help with their children's anger control. Parents frustrated by their children's constant screaming and yelling are looking for new ways to discipline their disruptive, noisy and quick-tempered youngsters.

Well-to-do parents will typically recognize their need for assistance once their punishments (time-out, spankings) have failed. Parents are sometimes pleasantly surprised to discover that simple approaches such as rewarding excellent conduct are effective.

What is the point of rewarding children for expected behaviour? When a youngster is rewarded for a behaviour, studies suggest that the child is more likely to repeat the activity. Consider this. Not long ago, your child was still learning to walk.

Children who fell repeatedly learned that their parents complimented their effort and cheerfully attempted to walk again. Even though they fell and scraped their knee, the youngster was commended once more for making an effort to learn to walk. After a month of being praised for an ability they lacked, something surprising occurs: (SUCCESS) The child learns to walk!

These are the fundamentals of education. To obtain what you desire, you must enjoy the road. Once something is no longer enjoyable, it becomes tedious, uninteresting and draining.

Children's anger management is that—if you want to change your child's behaviour, how can you convince them that the path will be enjoyable and exciting? Yes, you will need to use your imagination. However, there must be a way to compel your youngster to take out the garbage without prompting.

One method to demonstrate to your child that the journey is worthwhile and enjoyable is to offer them something they desire. Is your youngster in need of new shoes or have they been pleading with you to take them ice skating? Make a deal with them: if they keep their room spotless for a month, you'll take them ice skating.

I can hear some parents saying, "But what if my child continues to disobey?" Nothing. Parents must accept that children will naturally disobey their parents. It is a natural part of growing up and parents should understand that a rebellious child should not be used as an excuse to go crazy.

When parents resort to beating or screaming at children for defying their desires, they exacerbate an already difficult situation. At this point, parents must demonstrate their ability to deal with pressure.

After all, youngsters are constantly observing their parents' movements and mimicking them. Anger management for children is effective when the parent maintains a level head amid heated conflicts. Children's behaviour can be moulded through positive reinforcement and sentiments, so show them the way. Demonstrate to them that the journey is well worth the effort.

Many parents' primary concern when it comes to parenting is, "How do I establish effective anger control skills for children?" While there are other strategies for dealing with an angry child who refuses to obey their parent, these seven recommendations will go a long way toward assisting parents in regaining control.

1. Never demonstrate emotion — Demonstrating emotion just adds gasoline to a raging inferno. Children can pick up on their parents' furious feelings and respond with even greater anger.

2. Recognize your anger triggers—How do you feel just before you go into an angry tirade with your child? It's important to understand your tipping moments.

3. Accept responsibility for your actions—Parents who accept responsibility for their children's disputes are more likely to overcome the situation since they can devise strategies for resolving it.

4. R.e.l.a.x.—Parents who employ relaxation techniques mentally prepare themselves to deal with their children's undesirable mischievous actions. Their inability to become furious will have a calming effect on the child who sorely needs positive influences.

5. Seek solutions—Parents who seek answers for their children's anger management are more likely to find them. This may take the shape of professional counselling or a parenting support group.

6. Master the art of negotiation—Parents who understand that to obtain their desired outcome, they must make a concession understand how to elicit a positive response from their children.

7. Ignore poor behaviour—If your child's behaviour is persistent, it is because they have discovered that their poor behaviour garners your attention. Ignore the conduct if it is not life-threatening. Your child will discover that the conduct is ineffective.

Since anger management is not taught in today's high schools, parents only realize they want training in this important area when confronted with a 55lb, weeping, yelling, biting child who refuses to put back the Hershey's candy bar. On the other hand, parents are arming themselves with the knowledge necessary to restore order via patience and a desire to study.

(This page is intentionally blank)

Chapter 18

Anger Management as an Important Step toward Your Child's Bright Future

When the time comes for communion, children are often adept at this. While the anguish and guilt may weigh heavily on a child, this is not visible during a conversation. This can only be observed or felt through the child's behaviour.

They may conceal their emotions without expressing them openly. If the child is reserving a space for himself, he can be experiencing guilt. When they are angry, they will attempt to break their toys or yell and demonstrate their anger. These observations demonstrate that children express their emotions less verbally and more through movement.

When children display symptoms of anger, such as yelling and shouting or rolling on the floor, this indicates that they are experiencing some sort of difficulty. This is a big signal to the parents that the child requires assistance.

If no precautions are taken, this will escalate into a much larger problem in the coming days. You can easily discover an anger management program for children to help them overcome their anger issues. Parents must conduct the study to achieve the finest anger control, including trial and error with the guidelines.

Many materials exist that teach children various methods of anger management. You can locate them via the internet, which contains a wealth of information on this subject. Also, books and movies can be an excellent resource for teaching children how to handle their anger. If a parent is concerned about their child's anger-related behaviour, these sources may provide some relief.

There are various specialized programs available to assist children in coping with their emotions. Adult anger management or any other similar course will not help or benefit the child in any way. These programs are not developed enough to fit into a child's thinking. As a result, people cannot express their emotions honestly.

They can be unaware of what is occurring to them. You cannot expect the child to express his anger in front of a counsellor. To ascertain the source of his anger, you must follow particular measures in anger management for children.

Children enjoy being involved in sports and activities and involving them will aid them in managing their anger. Good values must be instilled in children appropriately through games and other more beneficial activities than individual sessions with an anger management counsellor.

A pleasant and appealing way for children to control their anger is to engage them in drawing, completing puzzles, or solving quizzes. Children should participate fully without being aware of the program.

Due to their lack of maturity, children cannot comprehend the notion of anger management. Considering that they are unaware of their emotions and cannot think and make quick decisions, for a child to grasp a good lesson, he must engage in logical thinking, which is impossible at their age and difficult to teach.

Anger control is crucial for children. A child must learn how to behave appropriately in different scenarios. The child must realize that while it is acceptable to be upset, they must not channel their anger in any way.

If a child is taught anger control skills at a young age, it will benefit them in the future. To effectively teach the child anger management skills, the activities must be thoroughly practiced. The parent must have the necessary patience to work with the child and observe the inevitable effects.

Some children appear to become adept at throwing a noisy temper tantrum independently—no training required. If, on the other hand, your youngster has not yet mastered the skill of a loud emotional explosion, consider one or more of the following training tips.

1. Demonstrate how it's done—with your actions. Whenever you become irritable, inform your children of how angry that other person made you. Make a note of all the instances the other person has disappointed you or mistreated you.

   This teaches children that your anger reaction is entirely the fault of the other person. Your example will educate your children to avoid accepting responsibility for their own emotions and to place blame for their out-of-control behaviours on others.

2. Generate a large number of no-win situations. Whenever feasible, provide your children with two or more behavioural options, neither of which they desire.

   For instance, "If you don't immediately switch off your favourite television show and clean your room, you can just go to bed now." Then be astonished when they complain! Become furious with yourself because you believe they will be grateful for the opportunity to cooperate. (Yes, indeed!)

3. Educate others about intolerance. Demonstrate to them that it is acceptable to feel furious when things do not go as planned. If your hamburger does not have pickles, fly off the handle at the counter worker, demanding your rights loudly and aggressively. Your children will recognize your strength and will begin to demand perfection—having everything as they want them. Otherwise!!!

4. Use your anger to outweigh your child's. When your child angers at you for whatever he believes you've done wrong, anger back with extra comments such as "How dare you." or "Do as I say or you will get it".or "You want something to weep about?"—"I'll give you something to cry about."

5. Recognize and reward angry behaviour. When your toddler throws tantrums at the check-out stand over a candy bar, give it to him. Allow your child to visit the park if he screams at you that he should be allowed to go because his friend is going (even if you have told him "No"). Allow her to stay up an extra half hour if she sobs and wails about not wanting to go to bed yet. Then you can be some to observe an increase in demand behaviours.

Perhaps you do not wish to teach your children this effective disruptive behavioural technique. What are your alternatives?

1) Keep an eye out for situations that are likely to set your child off. Then,

2) Behave in unexpected ways. Often, the element of surprise is all that is required to defuse a furious outburst. Then

3) Avert future angry reactions by studying how anger affects children (and how your children react to anger!) and how to assist your child in meeting their needs more peacefully.

Each child is unique. Each relationship between a child and parent is unique. No piece of advice for ANY parent-child interaction will work for EVERY family. The key to successful parenting is understanding why your children behave the way they do and how their behaviour benefits them.

Chapter 19

Simple Steps to Raising a Violent-Free Teen

Experts are hailing the unsettling behaviour of youngsters in the twenty-first century as a concerning trend among problematic youth. While this perception can be accurate, advocates for mental health believe parents may follow principles before problems reach an important stage.

They argue that the issues faced by children who disobey parental authority result from changes in both the outside world and family connections. For instance, we've seen a collapse in the discipline in recent years and a breakdown in familial authority. Family structures and roles are not as firmly defined as they formerly were. Often, parents are at odds. Also, peer engagement has overtaken family engagement.

Children are likely to witness their parents participate in abusive or corrupt behaviour in a society where law and order often spin out of control. Similarly, as violence and moral degradation become more prevalent, children begin to question their parents, Who are you to tell us what to do?

Consider how you are living and whether you have contributed to the world's devastation. While children often grow apart from their families as they become older, they still want direction.

At this period, parents are urged to demonstrate their adaptability and supervisory abilities. How parents enforce those regulations affects their children's success in adhering to them. The following are ten tips that, when followed religiously, will yield extraordinary results.

- Parental Responsibilities.

Rather than raising their children themselves, parents rely on teachers and other authority figures to fulfil the role of mother and father. Parents must become acquainted with their children's universe: their habits, friends, social network, and extracurricular activities to avoid conflict.

- Establishing the Rules.

While parents should set their standards, it is prudent to consult with other parents and possibly the school regarding prevalent views on curfews, drinking and other pertinent problems. You cannot always rely on youngsters to report honestly on regulations in other families. Thus, it is important to remember that because each family is unique, regulations will vary.

- Parents should adhere to the same set of guidelines.

Both parents should agree and support one another. Children will take advantage of any opportunity to exploit parental differences.

For instance: Roger, a fifteen-year-old with an intense libido, is informed by his macho father that it is usual for adolescent boys to have sex with many partners but his mother advocates for abstinence. Justin is completely perplexed as a result of disparity.

The solution: Parents should agree on a specific plan for dealing with difficult parts of their children's lives (sex, drugs, alcohol, rebellion). Reluctance and hesitation are intolerable. According to specialists, when a child perceives conflict, they are more likely to pit one parent against the other, resulting in a tremendous headache.

- Have a discussion with your children about the rules.

Explain your argument calmly and be prepared to provide evidence to support your claims. Remember that much has changed since you were your children's age. Pay close attention to your youngsters. Particularly the oldest, who often faces the most difficulties due to their role as a trailblazer for those who follow.

- Rules must be proportionate to the child's capacity for responsibility.

Not only physically but also emotionally, adolescence is a time of uneven development. While one 16-year-old can be mature enough to manage a flexible curfew, another may not be.

Parents must first assess their duties, expectations and motivations if regulations are not obeyed.

Are they aggravating the situation?

Are the demands unreasonable and unachievable?

Example:

Communal language.

What dialect do the parents speak?

If every remark is dirty or disgusting, there is a good chance their children will develop the same tendency—violent Conduct. Children do not inherit a propensity for violence. Other than that, it is acquired from parents and other adults. If you engage in violent conduct in front of your children, you might predict future difficulties.

- Make it clear to children who are in charge.

Parents who are fearful of their children and allow them to run amok are destined to encounter difficulties. Unlike previous generations, today's youngsters are protected by a bombardment of rules, making it impossible for parents to administer discipline.

Regardless of the legal process, parents should make it plain that they are in charge and that children must observe regulations as long as they are under their roof.

- Avoid confrontations with hostile individuals.

Create an atmosphere conducive to the expression of problematic events through positive reinforcement. If parents learn their daughter is abusing drugs, they must exercise restraint.

Other than that, they should maintain their composure and emphasize the consequences of substance usage. Following an explanation of your position, seek expert assistance. If the child refuses treatment, you as a parent are responsible for arranging her admission to a chemical dependency program within 36 hours.

- Never label a youngster as worthless.

Children, according to experts, are extremely impressionable. If a child is continually told he is worthless, he will act accordingly. As a result, he begins to live up to his image and becomes more prone to getting into mischief. Defiant conduct is often employed to garner attention or to push the boundaries.

- Always be understanding with your youngster.

Children respond well to fairness. It is acceptable to feel angry, though, if your concern for their safety prompts your anger. It is your responsibility to safeguard them; nonetheless, parents should refrain from intervening if their children commit a serious crime. If a youngster is convicted of stealing or destroying public property, they should face the appropriate punishment.

- Ensure that each child is treated equally.

Avoid paying excessive attention to one child at the expense of the other. Remember that each child is born with distinct abilities that are unmatched by anybody else.

Develop an appreciation for each child's talent and uniqueness. If parents adhere to these guidelines, perhaps misbehaving children will become a thing of the past rather than a future trend.

(This page is intentionally blank)

Chapter 20

How Children's Anger Management Can Help Prevent Suicide Attempts

Suicide among adolescents is a significant issue in this country. Every year, almost 132,000 children between the ages of 15 and 24 attempt suicide. That is the total undergraduate population of more than a dozen colleges attempting suicide each year.

However, the crisis does not end there. Every year, an additional 17,000 children aged 10 to 14 attempt suicide. It is the combined student body of nearly 15 middle schools.

One of the primary reasons for these juvenile suicide attempts is a lack of effective anger management skills. The children cannot cope with their circumstances. And due to their lack of anger management skills, they swiftly work themselves up to trying suicide. Parental ignorance of suicide warning signals exacerbates the situation and feeds the child's desire to commit suicide.

It is crucial to remember that almost all youngsters will exhibit warning symptoms before attempting suicide. Over 75% will even give you a verbal warning before committing suicide (basically to gauge your reaction).

It may not be as direct as "mom, I'm going to kill myself," but after the child commits suicide, you will always remember the words they spoke to you that could have helped you save your child's life.

If your child exhibits poor anger management skills, they can be at a high risk of attempting suicide. As a parent, you must get familiar with all possible suicide warning signals to determine whether your children will soon be at risk of self-harm. After ensuring their safety, you should teach effective anger management skills to prevent future suicide attempts caused by inadequate anger management abilities.

According to the most recent figures, suicide is the among the highest cause of death among 15 to 19-year-olds in the United States.

However, many academics believe that these figures are understated and that suicide may be the leading cause of death for that age group, as reliable statistics on suicide are difficult to get since many suicides are classified as accidental deaths.

Each year, suicide claims more young lives than cardiovascular disease, cancer, stroke, congenital disabilities, pneumonia, influenza and chronic lung disease combined. With such high suicide rates, we almost certainly all know someone who has attempted or committed suicide. However, as parents, what can we do to safeguard our children against suicidal thoughts or behaviours?

First, we must recognize that most suicidal young people do not wish to die; rather, they wish to alleviate their agony. What is this anguish, and how can we know whether our adolescent is having suicidal thoughts?

According to Dr. Heather Fiske, an expert on youth suicide and a psychologist at Toronto's Credit Valley Hospital, parents must "get familiar with the symptoms of sadness and how they relate to your child. Adolescents and adults experience depression differently."

Dr. Fiske continues, "Be on the lookout for abrupt changes in attitude, sleeping patterns, activity levels and wardrobe." Also, search for signs of severe depression triggered by abrupt changes, such as rejection by friends or a significant other.

These alterations should activate a parent's "there is an issue" section of the brain and, most importantly, take note if your child develops a fixation with death or begins discussing suicide, even if it is expressed through lines such as "You'd all be better off without me" or through artwork or writings containing images of death or the grim reaper.

Educational wellness and crisis response management company adds that parents should also be cautious of traumatic events in their teen's life (such as a close friend or relative's suicide), heavy alcohol and/or drug use and final arrangements, such as giving away prized possessions.

ACTIONS TO TAKE:

If you detect any of these warning flags in your teen's life, our initial reaction as parents is to fear and wonder what we did wrong. This does not just apply to you; it also applies to your spouse or ex-spouse.

As a single parent myself, I understand how difficult it is to maintain a comfortable relationship with an ex-spouse, especially when your child's life is at stake." Your ex-spouse can be aware of important information about your teen that you are unaware of at this moment.

When adolescents are suicidal, parents need to focus on the teen, not on previous parental failures. The adolescent requires immediate assistance. Suicide is not about our capacity to be good parents; suicide is about someone's inability to bear great suffering and recognize that it will lessen with time and aid."

Avoid overreacting; yet, if you do, you can always rectify the problem. Most importantly, do not procrastinate. Take action based on your feelings and seek the advice of a specialist who can assess the risk and if your child cannot see a professional, make an appointment for yourself."

However, while you, your teen, and the rest of your family should seek professional treatment first, do not fall into the trap of believing that it is no longer a family matter because this situation is extreme. Dr. Fiske advises her patients to "activate the household. They are an important component of treatment."

Dr. Fiske emphasizes the important role of parents in modelling self-care if they are to deal with the situation effectively. If parents support their children, they must go through their spectrum of emotions—guilt, humiliation, anger and shock. "Parents must set an example by seeking care for themselves.

Another part of caring for your suicidal adolescent includes remaining supportive and maintaining open lines of communication. It becomes natural for us to diminish others' sentiments with comments like, "I don't understand why you're unhappy; she (or he) was nothing but trouble and we didn't care for her (or him) anyhow."

Regardless of how you feel about the issue or difficulties causing your child extreme pain, the fact is that the issue is causing serious suffering to your teen and, even though your teen's current attention can be on the most recent significant unpleasant experience, this acute anguish is typically created by an accumulation of seemingly minor losses, not necessarily the most recent significant negative experience.

As parents, we must aim to be empathetic and sympathetic without being patronizing and to be available to listen at any time of day or night. Always be truthful to your child but never unkind. It is acceptable to express your emotions thoughtfully and constructively." Your adolescent needs to understand and internalize the fact that she is not alone during this important period.

Your teen needs to transition out of emotions of isolation and into a world filled with supporting resources and love. Providing support, getting assistance and maintaining optimism are the only methods for your family and teenager to survive this scenario.

(This page is intentionally blank)

Chapter 21

Parenting Techniques for Your Out of Control Adolescent

It appears as though every adolescent has an attitude; it's in their chemistry. They can't help themselves; their buddies do it and even you, the parents, do it occasionally. Some teenagers believe that the louder they yell, the more clearly they are heard. It's quite amusing; they will yell and repeat.

While your parents keep you cool, a large part of this is due to hormones. Accept the fact that the chicks are growing. They are maturing into adolescents. They are also feeling their freedom at this time. They are, in a sense, testing the waters.

By sitting down and conversing with them and I mean converse, no yelling permitted. Set examples do not compel but merely require a minute of their time. Maintain your composure and remember that you are the adult and flew off the handle all those years are being mocked. Therefore, now that they are older demonstrate to them how to communicate. They will pick up on things more quickly now that they are a little older.

If you desire a favourable outcome, you must be adaptable. If you want something from them, you must make a small contribution. Often, something simple can have the desired result; perhaps extend their curfew by a half-hour but inform them that they will face penalties if they violate the agreement. Put it on the line; they will now understand.

Your out-of-control adolescent may have demonstrated immense talent in their youth but has since waned. You can have lost some sleep over it, attempting to determine why it occurred.

You provided for all their resources, enrolled them in excellent schools and ingrained your culture in them, all to no avail. To be an exceptional parent, one must make sacrifices. Your goal has always been to set an example of a fit parent.

You must conduct yourself impeccably and advocate for high standards of living to expect the same of your adolescent. If your children are accustomed to receiving what they desire when they desire it, they can become verbally or physically hostile if their wish is not given quickly. Also, they may bully their parents and siblings.

Another significant source of aggression is parents who do not parent collaboratively, when one parent sides with the teen against the other, hostile and manipulative conduct are often the results because the child is bestowed with greater authority than the other parent.

In today's stressful world, you can undoubtedly hear the following from every parent of troubled teens: frustration; anger; grief, anguish, fear. Teens who were previously cooperative and pleasant become abruptly rebellious and unpleasant. Previously accessible children who were relatively easy to govern are suddenly seizing the initiative.

What is incorrect with this image?

Why do you fear this period in your children's lives as parents? These examples demonstrate the breadth of ways in which boundary concerns can impair relationships.

Boundaries are defined as anything that denotes a limit and is important for all of your relationships. Boundaries, alternatively referred to as rules, are how we protect ourselves in interactions with others and attempt to keep order in our lives. In most cases, parents failed to establish rules, enforce limits or violated their teen's boundaries.

These are some examples of boundary contexts.

- As a child, are you told that other people's needs are more important than yours?
- Are you rewarded for your selflessness and ability to please others?
- Are you taught to obey and embarrassed; were you harmed or punished for disobeying?
- Are you reprimanded for challenging authority?
- Did you grow up being taught to avoid conflict at all costs?
- Are you often instructed that you were accountable for another person's feelings or actions?

If you replied 'YES' to most of these questions, the cost was your sense of self which is the bedrock upon which borders are built.

Was your right to privacy protected?

Was it acceptable to have your own emotions and opinions?

Are you always encouraged to solve your problems and aid in the processor? Was someone constantly instructing you what to do and when to do it?

This type of encounter will affect your perception of where you end up and where others begin. Avoid passing on this baggage to your children.

Parents that have some tough teenagers must establish and enforce regulations. We tend to emulate our role models, often our parents, despite our best intentions when enforcing regulations.

When your child is doing what you want, you probably have no issue being a democratic parent.

However, you can be some that the first time your teen acts out, you will become the worst of both parents. Teens' needs continue to evolve as they mature. Do not be alarmed; it is common for adolescents to attempt separation from their parents at various phases of development.

Even under ideal circumstances, the teen years can be a struggle for any parent. If your children lack self-control or self-management skills, the consequences of their poor decisions at this stage of their lives can be catastrophic. It is feasible to take a stance and hold your position with some rules, even if you are initially fearful.

The adage "nothing changes unless something changes" is true. If you are unhappy with your out-of-control adolescent, you just have a few options. You can complain or wait for them to change or you can attempt to influence their behaviour. There is hope as long as both of you are alive.

The reality is that change must begin with you.

Chapter 22

Suggestions For Young Children's Anger Control

Toddlers and pre-schoolers are still developing their ability to manage their anger in public. Many parents struggle with child anger management and many appear hesitant to follow any advice provided by their children's grandparents, schools or community leaders. Tantrums and outbursts are unavoidable with children and parents must maintain their composure in these moments.

They must, however, be stern and consistent as well, as this assists in developing their child's discipline. This will also demonstrate to their youngster that they are taken seriously. Timeouts and distractions from irritated emotions are two strategies for managing young children's anger when they appear to be beginning a phase of furious conduct.

Teenage children's anger management tips

Diplomacy and tact are required while dealing with teenagers and enforcing discipline in this age range. You must be a good listener; inquire about your child's or son's experiences at school, with friends and with teachers. You must be aware of their difficulties and concerns.

If you see they are upset about something, maintain your composure and attempt to resolve the situation with focused questions and dialogues. You must communicate to your children clearly about behaviours that cannot be tolerated, such as slamming doors, throwing items or refusing to cooperate with household duties and homework.

You must be rewarding when dealing with adolescent anger. You can reward them with additional computer or television time for demonstrating self-control and appropriately processing their anger. Persuade your teens that you are on their side but do not allow them to become reliant on you.

As children age, you must ensure that they handle their emotions appropriately and in a socially acceptable manner. Raising children has grown more difficult than ever in the modern era.

Negative role models, selfish and self-centred pleasure, and eroding limits in our society drive youngsters to exhibit uncontrollable emotions, wreaking havoc on families, parents, relatives, and society. If your child exhibits signs of an out-of-control temper, follow the recommendations above and educate yourself on child anger management.

Imagine this scenario:

You received a call from school one day. It turned out that your adolescent child had just beaten up another person. This time, you're undoubtedly concerned. This would be thrice in three weeks and you were some something was gravely wrong with your child.

There is a strong possibility that your child is experiencing teenage anger, which has been increasingly prevalent in recent years. Each day, thousands of children become bullies, subject some of their friends to excessive peer pressure, curse and anger at parents, flee their homes or become involved in substance addiction and criminality.

As a parent, you undoubtedly hope there are strategies for dealing with it and assisting your teen before it is too late. There are:

- Take note of the trends.

Teenage anger is often defined as out-of-control or extreme anger. It is an outburst that often ends in physical, emotional or psychological injury to both the teen and others. This form of anger occurs often and sometimes for no apparent cause.

Nonetheless, parents should not dismiss a confrontation or dispute as a manifestation of adolescent anger. Your teen may be furious or annoyed by something. This sensation does not last for an extended period. Observe your teen's behaviour for a couple of weeks.

- Discuss the situation.

One of the first ideas for teens' anger control is to communicate with them. Determine the true source of their anger. Some teenagers engage in violent behaviour solely to garner your attention. Perhaps you've been preoccupied with other duties or believed they were old enough to live independently.

Many teenagers are amenable to the conversation, particularly if the perfect time and place are found. It is unquestionably worth pursuing.

- Conduct a crisis intervention.

On the other side, teens may not always want to listen to you. They believe what they are doing is perfectly acceptable. If this is the case, the next step is to request intervention for teenage anger management.

The facilitator determines how this is accomplished, although it is likely that the teen will be required to stay at a facility for days, weeks or months. It may take far longer if your teen is currently abusing substances. Drugs and alcohol can change the chemistry of the brain. Your son or girl requires detoxification.

- Create an environment that is caring and tranquil.

Make your home a comfortable place for everyone but especially your teen. Tension should be reduced. Surround your home with an abundance of love.

- Take into account the use of subliminal messaging.

Both teens and parents benefit from subliminal messages or affirmations. Their anger can be fuelled by the accumulation of unpleasant feelings within them. Affirmations can assist in reversing these negative thoughts.

Meanwhile, parents must learn how to deal with teen aggression properly. The affirmations will serve as a source of motivation.

When paired with other treatments for teen anger management, such as cognitive behavioural therapy, subliminal messages become even more successful. Never consider your teen to be a hopeless cause. If you give up, your son or daughter will likewise perish. Other than that, take the first courageous actions immediately.

Chapter 23

Educate Your Teen About What Works and What Doesn't Work with Anger Management

Assisting adolescents in managing their anger is important to their overall well-being. In some ways, it's also important to maintain the family and community's peace and safety. Troubled children with serious anger management issues often make life extremely difficult for other family members and pose a threat to the safety of others.

It's important to maintain perspective when teaching adolescents appropriate anger control skills. The reality is that anger is impossible to eradicate. A troubled adolescent feels even more upset when attempting to suppress their anger, which is an impossible task.

They often feel guilty and furious because they are unaware that anger is a natural human emotional response. There are therapeutic programs available for adolescents that provide effective ways for managing one's reaction to anger.

When you observe that your child has difficulty managing their anger, it is important to intervene early to avoid further self-inflicted injury. Some parents who are exhausted and fed up with dealing with an angry child believe that boot camp for teens can be the solution.

The issue is that juvenile boot camps emphasize anger suppression to escape punishment. Most teen boot camp programs were created to substitute for juvenile facilities, which is hardly conducive to a struggling child receiving the assistance he requires.

There are more troublesome teen camps and boarding schools that incorporate counselling into their programs. Teens can learn what causes their furious feelings throughout counselling.

Introspection and guided explorations can elicit information about each individual's unique trigger. Teens can identify and tackle these anger triggers in therapy, gaining a better understanding of why this is such a difficult subject for them.

Awareness is an important component in developing the ability to deal with a problem. Also, it provides teens with a good outlet for their feelings. Often, they do not fully comprehend it and comprehension leads to more constructive action.

Teens might also develop an awareness of the symptoms that indicate they are losing control of their anger. Individuals have physical reactions to strong emotions. Some individuals experience their hearts racing, jaws clenching, backs throbbing, or fists balling up. Teens who are more aware of the indicators of losing control have a better chance of regaining control.

Teens should also understand the consequences of uncontrollable anger. Apart from the harm it may cause to others and their property, there is also personal harm. Uncontrolled anger is like acid bubbling to the surface of a container.

The container is the first thing that is destroyed. Uncontrollable anger can result in hyperacidity, ulcers, back discomfort and hypertension, among other complications. Not to mention the emotional toll it has on the individual.

Assisting a child displaying signs of anger, such as rolling on the ground and aggressive behaviour, is important to avoid future problems caused by the same upsetting situation and to assist them in becoming aware of their undesirable behaviour, which is necessary for anger management programs to work.

Anger management programs for children are distinct from those for adults, as discussing or discussing the subject may not be conducive to the less mature minds of children, in addition to their difficulty verbalizing their feelings; thus, with a little bit of research and experimentation with various resources on the subject and experimenting with various techniques for controlling and diverting anger in a positive direction.

Among the most useful resources for children's anger management are different books written by prominent psychologists and films and websites on the internet that inform, educate and guide people through the maze of information available on the subject of anger and how to best address the issue to help children and their families.

Children's anger management programs are specifically created for their benefit. In contrast, adult anger management programs focus on group involvement, talking and discussions, which is not the greatest method to achieve results from intellectually immature children. Thus, the most effective method of doing a child's anger management therapy is through a series of enjoyable and exciting activities.

Many of these specially developed anger management programs for children are built around entertaining activities that involve them in games that reinforce positive values and teach them about sharing and desirable behaviour.

Children are given colouring, puzzles and quiz worksheets representing angry events with possible negative and positive outcomes, emphasizing the positive outcomes of effective anger management. This mixes fun and activities for children's anger control.

For children, a play-based method of instilling good values and redirecting anger is preferable to a one-on-one session with an anger management counsellor. This is because worksheets and games methods work well at eliciting acceptable behaviour traits in children, whereas designing lesson plans that require logical thinking is reserved for adults.

Anger management for children is important for instilling desirable and acceptable social conduct and assisting them in overcoming their problem behaviours to develop into successful teens and adults in their future lives.

A proven approach of child anger management therapy is to determine why a child is upset and exhibiting anger negatively, attempting to reduce the reaction, and teaching constructive ways to express anger through repetitive activities.

Chapter 24

Simple Ways to Help Your Children Grow Into Happy, Confident Adults

Being a parent in the modern era is not an easy undertaking. With an abundance of negative external factors, it is more difficult than ever to raise a child with good self-esteem and the necessary self-reliance later in life. Fortunately, there are five components you can implement immediately to assist your children in developing into joyful, self-assured individuals.

a. Maintain a Firm Yet Just Discipline

As furious as you can become when your children misbehave, speaking in a low, authoritative tone is important, emphasizing their bad behaviour rather than the children themselves.

Also, before disciplining your children, ensure that they understand why they are being punished, know your expectations and understand how they should behave in the future. Rather than telling them to "stop moaning," for example, instead, "please speak clearly so that I can understand what you're saying."

b. Strengthen Their Self-Esteem

If you observe your child having wrong or unrealistic beliefs or expectations about themselves or others, correct their thinking immediately to prevent these mistaken impressions from becoming a reality for your child.

Allow your children to try and discover what they enjoy, like and are good at without the constant pressure of winning.

By encouraging children to pursue activities and talents that align with their strengths, you can help them develop their self-esteem and personality and inspire them to consider what they want to be when they grow up.

c. Set an Excellent Example

Ensure that you work on your self-esteem, as being overly important of yourself may result in your child copying your way of thinking. Also, responding to difficulties in an optimistic, solution-oriented manner teaches children that problems are temporary and can be resolved.

If you find yourself acting in less-than-ideal ways or speaking in anger, recognize your error and seek forgiveness. Admitting mistakes and accepting responsibility teaches youngsters that it is acceptable to be imperfect and that taking responsibility for one's actions is important.

d. Praise Them

Praise your children not for a job well done but for their willingness, intention and effort. Praise youngsters as well when you observe them making wise decisions. It's important to recognize positive actions by mentioning particular items you enjoyed. For instance, you can say, "I'm pleased of you for making a wise choice and electing to complete your homework before asking permission to play with your friends."

e. Assist Your Children in Managing Stress

By being sensitive and compassionate, you can assist your child in developing appropriate coping mechanisms for stress.

When you observe your child struggling, acknowledge the emotions they can be experiencing with a sympathetic statement such as, "It's upsetting and frustrating to have your friends cancel on plans you were looking forward to," or "It's upsetting and frustrating to have your friends cancel on plans you were looking forward to."

This enables your child to feel supported by you, alleviates bad feelings and frustrations and enables them to develop a greater awareness of (and hence a greater ability to convey) their feelings.

Effective parenting involves love, attention and total commitment. Expressing your sentiments to your children, particularly how much you care about and love them, will not only aid in their healthy growth but also aid in the formation of a lifelong link between you and your children.

(This page is intentionally blank)

Chapter 25

How Children's Anger Management Worksheets Work

Anger is a universal feeling that everyone, including children, experiences. While it is sad that children must deal with the negative consequences of anger issues, it is important to work with them and get them involved in an anger management program.

Lack of ability to manage children's anger will certainly support a pattern of anger throughout their adolescent years and into adulthood. When you notice a child's behaviour changing, particularly their anger, it is important to counsel them and refer them to anger management therapy. Regrettably, anger disorders are such a pervasive problem in our culture. It's even more tragic to consider that youngsters and teenagers must deal with this issue.

Fortunately, individuals such as doctors and professional management counsellors are interested in children who struggle with anger. As a result, many support organizations and anger management programs have been created expressly for this age range.

Apart from support groups and programs, there are additional options available to youngsters who struggle with anger. Anger management worksheets for children appear to be one item that appears to be beneficial.

Children are asked to work through their anger issues using anger management workbooks. Offering circumstances and episodes involving anger, these management worksheets expose children to similar difficulties and teach them how to work through them.

Children appear to communicate effectively with colouring sheets and many types of problem-solving activities such as puzzles. Providing anger management worksheets for children is a prudent decision that will undoubtedly be positively received by the children concerned.

Children who are coping with anger difficulties can be unaware they have a problem. Children are continually learning as they grow and they are not expected to comprehend every scenario, including their unique feelings and experiences, in their innocence. Finding successful strategies for treating their child's anger issues can be difficult, depending on their age.

Anger management worksheets for children are techniques that most children will respond to. Children are typically eager to learn and explore new situations. Anger management worksheets for children can be incorporated into a child's program without emphasizing its purpose. A child can be working through their issues without realizing they are being targeted for their anger issues.

Children of all ages enjoy fun and activities. Children would respond much better to the underlying management if they were compelled to sit with an advisor and address their difficulties if given pleasant and fascinating management worksheets.

While children may not always articulate their feelings, they can unknowingly deal with their anger issues through workbooks. If a person is looking for anger management worksheets for children, they should contact their local community medical institution.

Administering to youngsters who have anger issues can be difficult and take thought and inventiveness. Typically, a child's thinking is not evolved enough to deal with powerful sensations of anger.

They express these emotions in their unique youthful way, often through acting out or throwing a tantrum. Unaware of these behavioural responses' intricacies, children are inadequately equipped to elaborate or convey their sentiments. Finding programs and tools to help children control their anger effectively will certainly need forethought and well-thought-out programming.

When developing an anger management program for children, the creator must consider the activities and exercises that will engage the children. Placing a child in a support group or scheduling an appointment with a psychiatrist is unlikely to yield positive outcomes.

Because the child does not comprehend their anger, sharing or discussing it with others can be difficult. Children might benefit from worksheets and activities that are tailored to their issues.

Worksheets, colouring pages and puzzles are all familiar to children. These kinds of activities are utilized daily in the classroom. It would make sense to incorporate management skills into these endeavours. Worksheets for anger control might be disguised as enjoyable and fascinating.

These worksheets could teach children systems and strategies for managing their anger to understand and respond to it. Utilizing familiar situations in colouring sheets or comparable terms in puzzles might assist a youngster in resolving anger issues without involving the position.

Children enjoy activities and having a good time. Apart from worksheets, incorporating games into a child's anger management program can be beneficial. Many issues with anger in children stem from jealously and competition. Playing games that teach youngsters healthy peer interaction and fair play will affect their conduct.

Teaching youngsters that it is acceptable to play games and not always win is beneficial for their behavioural development. Creating activities that incorporate role-playing may help children understand that they cannot constantly be the centre of attention. Anger management for children can be taught in different ways that are both useful and pleasant.

When children exhibit indicators of anger and distress, anger management worksheets can be used to help identify the underlying issue. Creating a list of possible causes of their anger and having them read through it to determine which statements pertain to them can be beneficial in helping children who have anger issues.

Simple sentences based on ordinary difficulties that a child may meet can be used in these anger management worksheets. Children may not understand the purpose of these worksheets, yet they can be contributing relevant information that may aid in the treatment of their problem.

To build an effective anger management worksheet for children, it is necessary to understand how a child's mind works and what fascinates them and utilize this knowledge to create an impressive anger management program for children.

Chapter 26

Ways to Regain Control of Your Child's Anger Issues

Children's anger management is one area of parenting where well-to-do parents freely confess they need assistance. Last week, I spoke with a mother who has a six-year-old son whom she described as "hell on earth." When she was questioned about what made him this way, she responded with a lengthy list of transgressions he had done in the preceding week.

On Monday, he struck his younger brother in the head with an Xbox controller, got into an altercation with a small child over a grilled cheese sandwich on Tuesday, and stole $3 from his mother's purse to purchase candy from the school vending machine on Wednesday.

The frustrated expression on her face indicated that she might easily have continued the story for another week, so I interrupted her to ask her the following question. "How have you interpreted his behaviour"?

She gave me a perplexed expression, so I repeated the question, "What has your child's conduct taught you?" After a few moments of deliberation, she glanced at me and answered, "nothing." That is where the fault rests, as she has been squandering an excellent opportunity to learn more about her son.

Her subsequent inquiry was, "How do you learn from such hopeless and desperate circumstances?" You learn the same way you do in any other situation by taking baby steps. To begin, I urged her to monitor the scenario the next time an emotional outburst occurs.

Take note of the time of day since he can be weary, eliciting negative undesirable emotions. I instructed her to take note of his level of activity just before he exhibits aggressiveness. This may indicate that he is bored and violence can be his method of attracting attention.

Children are not born with harmful habits; they develop them over months and years of growing up in the presence of parents, siblings, electronic devices and friends, among others.

If a parent wants to succeed in child anger management, they must first understand their child's feelings without responding. Understanding what makes your child tick helps equip you to moderate any violent situation.

Nowadays, there is a top ten list for almost everything: Top ten strategies to lose weight, Top ten ways to cook wonderful chicken and Top ten websites to visit in 2009. This chapter discusses child anger management and the Top 10 strategies to regain control.

Are these Top Ten Methods fool proof? True and false

Yes, because with practice, dedication and patience, this Top 10 list will almost always work. No, because parents who lack practice, devotion and patience will fail. Why?

Because teaching children anger management skills is not a one-night stand, established patterns do not change overnight. Without further ado, here is a top ten list of ways for parents to regain control.

- Teach your child to count to ten

I realize this is a very common method of controlling anger but it is one of the most effective methods of combating aggression in youngsters.

- Understand anger

Furious feelings are a natural and healthy part of a child's development; if parents search for the lessons from angry moments, they can be pleasantly pleased to learn something about their child.

- Close your eyes

Parents should close their eyes and dream before reacting to bad feelings. What do you fantasize about? Who knows dream about anything that gets your mind off your current circumstances.

- Make contact with someone

The only thing that is worse than anger is unspoken anger. Anger must be conveyed in a manner that allows for venting. Contact a friend or family member who is prepared to provide an ear. This provides you with another individual who can offer sound advice on how to control your child's anger.

- Play

Playing with your child provides an opportunity for your child to make new friends. It will decrease the likelihood of your youngster displaying aggression in the first place. A youngster who is engaged in play is a happy child.

- Teach your youngster effective anger management techniques.

If you educate your child on managing their anger, you will equip them with the tools necessary to pull themselves out of a mental bind. A youngster can never be too young to acquire self-control.

- Turn off the television

A study found that youngsters who spend excessive time watching television, particularly epically violent television shows, are more prone to display anger and aggressiveness toward others.

- Admit fault

When disputing with a child, remember that parents are the adults regardless of what is said, has been said or will be said. Admit your faults to accomplish one goal: peace.

- Relax

How to relax? I'm not sure because everyone is unique but relaxing for me entails resting in a hot tub and soaking away the day's mental tension. After a steamy bath, you'll see the humour in a child who spent the afternoon brightening the walls.

- Participate

Yes, I am aware that this was number five but it is important to a child's development. When your child begins to act aggressively, attempt to calm the situation by engaging them in their favourite game—what a wonderful method to transform tears into laughs.

Chapter 27

Preventing Child Anger

Children often imitate their peers' poor behaviour. This is a natural element of a child's learning process. It is designed to instil social skills in children through play. The purpose of this activity is for the parent and child to interact through role play.

The parent must allow the youngster to take the lead in this game and gently correct their behaviour as needed. It is important never to inform a child that they are doing something incorrectly, resulting in low self-esteem.

Parents should recognize that they are their child's primary influence and role models. You must always be mindful of your behaviour in the presence of your child. Consider "would I want my child to behave the same way I do?" Being aware of this will greatly assist you in encouraging your child's good behaviour. This is important when it comes to child anger management.

- The Appropriate Reaction

Never take a negative stance in response to your child's temper tantrum or anger. Observe deep breaths and avoid being hasty with your discipline. This instant discipline is often excessively severe and results in your youngster harbouring justified hatred toward you. Take a break and consider your options. This will result in the proper application of discipline.

- Prevent Boredom

Often, boredom results in mischief. Once again, this is a natural reaction. Children require and desire education, therefore provide them with activities. Eventually, your youngster will discover amusement on his own, without your intervention. This is your objective.

- When To Reward And When Not To

This is among the most important approaches for managing child anger. Always reward positive behaviour, not negative behaviour. Parents often offer something to a child who is misbehaving, such as a treat or a toy, in an attempt to settle them down. This is a grave error. This will be interpreted as a reward for the youngster's angry display and hence the child will continue to exhibit this behaviour.

- Establish Boundaries

The parent must always establish a child's boundaries. This instils a sense of security in a child. This does not, however, prevent the child from testing them. The key is to remain unflinching. Once boundaries are established, they must be followed. While it may not feel like way, creating limits demonstrates to the child that you care about them.

Parenting can be challenging but there are ways that parents can master it. Never be hesitant to inquire about other parents' experiences. Many parents are natural-born experts in child anger control.

If your child can control his anger, the best thing you can do is reward them with your undivided attention. This will demonstrate to your child that they are valuable to you and that focusing exclusively on their anger will only make them feel worse.

You can easily assist your youngster in becoming calmer and refocusing. You can instruct your child to inhale deeply and count to ten. If they remain furious, instruct them to continue counting or to perform some backward counting. This will undoubtedly divert their attention away from being upset.

At times, a child cannot express their frustration verbally. The best course of action is to provide your child a piece of paper and a pen and let them write or draw how they feel or why they are angry in the first place.

Attempt to dissipate the child's anger. This is another excellent piece of advice you can give your youngster. Allow your youngster to play pillow fights with you to begin. Alternatively, you can ask your youngster to walk or ride their bike with you. This will undoubtedly distract them from their anger.

We must comprehend, practice and teach our children important anger management skills to manage their anger effectively. In our schools, homes and institutions, we have witnessed the devastation caused by suppressed anger. Let's learn to cope with it efficiently now so that there are no unexpected occasions in your family's life.

Recognize your child's anger and her legitimate right to be furious. When you're angry, the last thing you want to hear is that you have no reason to be angry or that you should "stop acting that way." You want your voice to be heard. You want to vent your anger because it is motivated by a sense of injustice of some kind.

Often, anger is motivated by pain or fear. Anger stems from a sense of love being withheld in some form. It can take on different guises. You can believe you have a convincing explanation for anger at first glance - yet beneath the anger is always a concealed fear or anguish.

By talking it out, you can assist your child in confronting their fear or pain. Investigate the source of the problem. If your child is yelling, do not respond with yelling; instead, sit quietly and listen, bringing calm and understanding to the issue. Allow your child to abuse you with assaults but understand that occasionally a few lines of outburst can be necessary to keep the cork from popping. Then, inhale deeply and talk it out.

Assure your child that anger is OK. Rather than attempting to stop it, assist your child in learning to communicate effectively and assure her that you will always listen as any kind person would. Often, talking it out diffuses the anger, even if you have to return to the subject many times. Continue to work on it until it is resolved while staying loving, kind and respectful at all times.

Demonstrate effective anger management to your child. At times, we are all furious. When you begin to feel furious, take a deep breath and exhale deeply, centring your being before continuing to express why you are upset. This will become more natural as you practice. If you become furious, do not believe that you are a horrible parent or a bad example.

Children require good role models for emotional control and if you attempt to conceal or conceal anger, your child will sense it nonetheless, making your efforts ineffective. Be truthful, be open and take the opportunity to grow from each event and emotion.

Remember that compassion and respect are necessary components of healthy partnerships. If relationships are not founded on compassion and respect, anger will inevitably surface.

Assist your youngster in comprehending this universal fact about all relationships. Even if your child dislikes someone, they need to be respectful and as kind as possible. Where basic decency and respect are lacking, complications ensue.

You cannot always agree with your child and may even disapprove of some of their choices. However, as long as you show compassion and respect to your child and accept them for who they are, anger issues can and will be resolved. Remember that you do not have to approve of your child's personality. It is important, though, that you accept your child for who they are.

Acceptance is important, even when you disagree. Your child is an individual and some parents spend years and shed many tears learning that acceptance is the bedrock. Contrary to popular belief, disagreement is acceptable; rejection is not.

Explain to your child how you deal with your anger. To assist in releasing anger, you can employ prayer, meditation, deep breathing, physical activity and talking it out. While prayer and meditation are more long-term options, deep breathing, exercise and talking it out are immediate and short-term ways to diffuse anger.

My ten-year-old child has discovered that deep breathing is particularly important before discussing the matter and conveying his point of view. He also utilizes prayer to ground himself and feels more balanced and capable of dealing with his various emotions.

He also drew a poster for his room some time ago that reads, "If I become too upset, I walk away from the situation." This has served as a reminder to him to take a pause and cool down when necessary.

Occasionally, children do not appear to understand why they are particularly furious. They may experience an accumulation of anger due to seemingly few events.

By being a caring, supportive parent and recognizing past anger habits, you can assist your child in resolving these minor difficulties one at a time. Also, if you spend time with your child asking her to "feel into the anger" and discussing it calmly, melancholy will often surface, which you can explore together.

Peeling back the layers of anger can often feel like peeling an onion but anger is occasionally like that. Continue peeling. Continue to be there for her through the tears, the ranting and the upset and let her know that you accept and love her regardless of what happens and that you will get through this together.

Finally, you serve as a role model for your child. If you express your anger in an inappropriate manner, your child will as well. As you teach the anger control strategies, practice them yourself. You wish to teach your child how to resolve little conflicts so that anger does not develop into a habit or becomes entrenched as a teenager.

Of course, as a loving parent, you can address all forms of anger by returning to these principles but early intervention is preferable. Maintain your composure and concentration on your role as guide and instructor rather than becoming personally offended by any incident. Assume the role of observer and assistant.

Finally, true love is about personal devotion to one another through both the easy and difficult times. Anger is a natural feeling that does not have to be a source of contention within a family. Breathe deeply and employ love, respect, and kindness to heal anger and establish a healthy, loving family bond.

Chapter 28

Strategies For Assisting Your Children In Developing Self-Controlled Emotional Selves

Change is difficult for everybody but it is especially challenging for children! Their brains are not fully formed in the "thinking" department and their emotions are immature.

Although children are born with unique inclinations, the emotional environment in which they are reared affects them. Thus, parents are ultimately accountable for two distinct types of emotional inheritance: natural and nurtured.

Genetic predispositions are more challenging to diagnose and control. Environmental factors, on the other hand, are more adjustable. Parents are often aware that their emotions, such as anger, affect their children's emotional development. Many parents seek assistance in re-establishing emotional balance and self-regulation.

As parents acquire new abilities and evolve, their children do as well. However, parents aren't the only ones who can benefit from developing new abilities for modifying behaviour. Children can also develop anger management abilities. The following are five strategies for assisting your children in developing self-controlled emotional selves:

Identify emotions: Create or purchase a set of feeling cards that depict emotion-filled faces alongside emotion-filled phrases. Settle down with your youngster and ask him to choose 3-6 cards that accurately depict his emotions.

Allow him to explain, "I was furious when the teacher told me to stay inside during recess while everyone else went outside." Do this a couple of times a week to help your youngster combine both feeling and expressing language. Assure that you listen to and accept your child's sentiments.

Due to the natural nature of the fight or flight response, we cannot ignore the want to express our emotions in specific ways. When we are furious, we may feel compelled to strike or yell. It is important to reassure children that they are not crazy for feeling this way.

It is also important for children to understand that fighting or fleeing is not always necessary when distressed. Role-playing with them is one approach to teach alternate emotional choices. Choose an emotion card and demonstrate how your body reacts when it sees the term.

Make it a reality. Then demonstrate alternate behaviours that correspond to that same emotion. Then let your youngster role-play various acts in response to various emotions. As you brainstorm alternate behaviours or thoughts, jot them down on the reverse of each feeling card.

Self-Talk: Children are exposed to self-talk from an early age. Self-talk often reflects the emotional tone of the child's environment. One may live in an extremely good atmosphere and so be able to make positive remarks inside.

Self-talk can mirror the experience of a bad environment. For example, an internal dialogue in which it is stated, "Mommy is very vindictive. This is completely unjust. "I despise life" can be transformed into "I need to improve." I am insufficient; nobody understands me."

Children occasionally struggle to become conscious of their self-talk. I attempt to assist them by outlining the positive and negative aspects of self-talk.

To help them understand the notion of self-talk, I recommend watching the film The Emperor's New Groove. One of the characters, Kronk, exhibits his positive and negative self-talk by wearing an angel on one shoulder and the devil on the other.

Throughout the film, the angel and devil have a running dialogue, similar to our self-talk. Children often identify with this, which facilitates discussion of their internal conversation.

Emotional Eclipse: "Catharsis" is a term that refers to the process of emotional purification. Historically, people were urged to hit pillows when they were upset as a cathartic release method.

However, upon further reflection and analysis, it was discovered that striking a pillow in anger increased angry behaviour!

Indeed, it was discovered that when people relaxed, reflected and refocused, and furious sentiments were quelled and diminished. When I teach children how to choose calm conduct in response to frustration, I refer to it as an emotional eclipse. Using my mood cards, I demonstrate to them how anger can transform into calm.

To assist your youngster in mastering the emotional eclipse technique, create a list of furious versus calm behaviours. Demonstrate how they may overcome a negative emotion by positive conduct and eventually have greater control over their emotions.

I make children dance or hop up and down to music to display behavioural control. They experience a boost in energy, similar to how they do when they are upset. Their heartbeat quickens. Their bodies begin to heat up.

Then I turn off the music and we sit quietly, breathing deeply and conversing slowly. Their heart rate slows down. Their bodies begin to chill. Children then comprehend how they might overcome their furious sensations through the use of soothing practices.

Children learn via modelling. How do you deal with your grief?

When you're angry, what do you do?

If your actions discourage your children from acting, you must address your concerns. You can explain to them that you, too, have problems remaining cool when furious and that you'd like to learn how to control your reactions. If you behave quietly in the face of anger, be sure to convey how you maintain your composure.

Discuss your internal processes with your children. You could add, "Today at the grocery store, I felt quite sad. I was pressed for time and the cashier took advantage of me. I had to return to the room and convince her to redo the transaction. I didn't want to be impolite, so I had to suppress my anger.

I kept convincing myself that she didn't intend to do it. Getting angry does not help. I'm not going to get anywhere faster by being upset." Parents exert a significant influence on their offspring. Ascertain the efficacy of your impact.

These tips have aided many parents in their efforts to educate, coach and counsel their children. Remember that educating your children about the world of emotions equips them with the skills necessary to care for themselves, have good relationships and achieve their life goals.

Chapter 29

Tips To Help Kids With Anger Problems

Anger is a common feeling anyone can experience, even kids. However, it can be upsetting when this explosive emotion has already taken over and grabbed the most out of you. This is why understanding how to manage anger issues is extremely vital.

But do you realize that even kids can have anger problems? Yes, just like adults, young children can feel the enormous strain that can force them to break and become violent.

Proven a thousand times before, this may be very distressing, especially since aggressive tendencies can adhere to a youngster. It can evolve to something that can offer genuine hazards to the child and the people around him.

Luckily, there are strategies to help kids with anger problems. Some of the things you can do to help your child deal with this kind of difficulty are the following:

- Set a good example.

Kids learn better by what they observe, so make sure you also check your fits. Set a good example by regulating your anger effectively.

A fantastic approach to achieve this is by adopting the exit technique when things start to become too heated around the household (particularly because anger is extremely contagious) (especially since anger is quite contagious). If you're getting upset with them around, make sure to remove yourself from the situation, so you can prevent a large conflict that will not help your kids with anger problems.

- Teach them calmness.

By teaching your children how to manage their anger calmly, you may assist them in resolving their difficulties productively. The most effective method to accomplish this is through example. By demonstrating appropriate calm in the face of difficult conditions and situations, you may ensure that you can assist your children in resolving their anger issues.

- Discuss their emotions with them.

Typically, children are frustrated because no one will listen to what they have to say. Therefore, to assist children with anger issues, speak with them about what irritates them and how they feel. Additionally, you can assist them in establishing an emotional vocabulary that will aid them in better expressing their emotions.

- Promote positive conduct.

You may tell whether your child is ahead of his anger difficulties when he or she is already demonstrating constructive problem-solving skills. To further encourage this, ensure that such behaviour is acknowledged. This will undoubtedly promote such behaviours, helping your youngster to develop more fully.

- One type of anger management training considers a fundamental fact of nature:

Energy may be transformed into other forms. For example, fossil fuels can be transformed into electrical energy. When we move, potential energy transforms into kinetic energy.

The trick is to discover a way to make this conversion enjoyable and accessible.

Assisting your child in channelling excess energy, tension, or anger into something beneficial is simple with art. Children are born with an innate capacity for creative expression. Numerous individuals merely require the space, time, and materials necessary for creative transformation to occur.

- Make selection the major objective of this exercise.

Giving the reluctant child a choice is the most effective method of eliciting cooperation. Prepare as many supplies as possible, including paper mache, paint, craft dough, crayons, brushes, pencils, plastic spoons, potatoes, forks, paper, newsprint strips, and Bristol board.

- Allow space and time for the child's creative inclinations.

The rear yard of the house or a hose-cleanable deck is ideal for generating a yearning to create something from your heart.

The key is to give the child space - space to work with the materials, space to experiment and play with what is in front of him or her, space to ponder, and to allow ideas to gel, and even space to stop and restart. We must immediately discard the one-hour arts and crafts session concept; no one can work creatively under time constraints.

- Express gratitude and encouragement openly and frequently.

You are not preparing your child for a career in the arts at the Academy of the Arts. You are providing an outlet for the energetic self.

Positive reinforcement is the most effective method of keeping this self-occupied. Any work, regardless of its stage of completion, is deserving of praise. The youngster is creating something out of nothing, which is remarkable in and of itself.

Positive comments assist the youngster in establishing a link between a certain action and his emotional condition. You want him or her to commit to this connection for the rest of their lives.

- Play calm classical music or joyful children's songs in the background.

Numerous studies have established that music has a profound effect on our emotions. Researchers observed that the positive emotions evoked by cheerful music could positively influence blood vessel function. The emotion of joy evoked in listeners dilates or expands the blood vessels, allowing for more oxygenation in the body.

- Exhibit your child's artwork.

Convert your residence into an art gallery. Nothing boosts self-esteem like seeing one's work showcased and praised. My granddaughters' artwork is displayed on my refrigerator and on the walls that go up and down the stairs in my house. I put them inside frames so that my house becomes a genuine art gallery for their creations.

- If possible, create with your children.

I enjoy creating my artworks with the children. Being present gives the experience a whole new depth. I'm not only supervising them; I'm fully involved in their play.

It's not only enjoyable for me (it helps me seem ten years younger); it's important for my artistic development. They make excellent recommendations. When given the opportunity, children make the best art critics.

Anger management does not have to be a high-intensity form of training. Through art, anger management may be enjoyable, focused, and transformative.

With these recommendations, you can be certain that you can do something to assist children experiencing anger issues. Bear in mind, however, that positivism in the household is the most critical component for effectively managing the condition.

(This page is intentionally blank)

Conclusion

Teenage years are important to a children's development. Unfortunately, these are the years during which children face some of their most difficult interactions. This stage of a child's life can take them down different courses, not all pleasant. Teenagers who are forced to deal with adversity often lash out.

Developing a risky attitude is common in a large proportion of adolescent children. When adolescents develop anger emotions and begin to act out, it can be time to seek out anger management for teen children.

As a child, coping with the many situations that constantly present themselves can be emotionally taxing. This strain elicits a wide range of emotions and thoughts, including anger.

When someone pushes someone's buttons, anger is a natural reaction. However, it is what an individual does with those feelings that make a difference. Anger management teaches self-awareness and willpower to adolescent youngsters. Anger is a very strong emotion.

When anger is handled incorrectly, it can result in extremely damaging and uncomfortable acts or emotions. Developing the ability to control these emotions at a young age will undoubtedly impact adult life. When there is evidence of anger difficulties in adolescent children, it is vital to seek anger management.

Managing anger is all about empowerment, mastering the ability to assess the situation and make informed choices rather than acting on impulse. While it is easy to attack the first hint of opposition, exercising self-control and acting rationally and logically requires self-control.

This may seem like a lot to ask of adolescent teenagers, but it is possible with the appropriate attitude. This may entail individual counselling, support groups or attendance at a retreat for teens with anger issues. While the path to success is important, the ultimate result is what matters most.

Self-awareness is a necessary component of teaching young adult anger management for teen children since it teaches the individual that they can examine events that make them furious.

Encouraging the teen to pay attention to their feelings throughout vexing occasions is important for their anger control. Assisting them in recognizing the value of thinking during a true hostile interaction will benefit the environment. A teen who is prone to anger also requires instruction in self-control.

While it is possible to quantify the distressing scenario, self-control plays a role in the teenager's behaviour. Encouraging them to pause and reflect, pause for a few seconds between their initial sentiments of anger and their reaction, will almost always result in great outcomes.

When confronted with a provocative scenario, self-awareness and self-control go hand in hand. Anger management for adolescent children encourages the youngster to examine their feelings, the circumstance and the true source of the antagonism.

Taking a few seconds to meditate on these concepts in their mind will influence their action or response. While managing children who have anger issues might be difficult, many resources are available to assist with teen child anger management.

While teaching child anger management skills can be challenging, the results are well worth the effort. If the struggle results in protecting a child from danger and pain, it is unquestionably worthwhile.

Best of Luck!

www.ingramcontent.com/pod-product-compliance
Lightning Source LLC
Chambersburg PA
CBHW052033150726
48002CB00002B/588
9798215174906